BEEF STEW FOR 2500

Feeding Our Navy from the Revolutionary War to the Present

RUDY SHAPPEE

Published by South Jetty Publishing
7243 Viar Avenue
San Diego, California 92120

Printed and bound in China

ISBN 978-0-9669637-1-7

Book design by Jo-Lin Govek
ChampCohen Design Associates
Del Mar, California
www.champcohen.com

Official photos and drawings courtesy of The Library of Congress, Department of the Navy, and the U.S. Naval Institute.

DEDICATION:

To those who come from on the land,

To make their way upon the deep,

Who share their bounty,

One with the other,

Upon the decks of ships at sea.

CONTENTS

Introduction

Since the opening of the U.S.S. Midway Museum in 2004, volunteers and staff have been asked by our numerous guests how the ship's cooks could have possibly served enough food to keep the crew of 4,500 men healthy and able to perform the strenuous work necessary aboard an aircraft carrier during extended periods at sea. The *Midway* staff's first response was to develop "Talking Points" our Docent Corps could use in explaining this process. But our guests wanted more. "How many pounds of beef go into beef stew for 2500 men?" one person asked. "How do you cook enough for everyone without having too many leftovers, or not enough for those who are at the end of the mess line?" asked another. While the answers to questions like these were left to the experience as well as the creativeness of individual staff members faced by curious guests, the rest of us struggled to fill this void in our museum's story.

While I was working on the museum book, *Midway Memories*, with Scott McGaugh, the *Midway* Museum's publicist, our discussions turned again and again to the potential solution for "the food story." Should we build an exhibit containing recipe cards in the galley area? What about a listing of a typical week's menus? How many volunteers would we need in the galley to explain away the mysteries of food preparation aboard such a large ship, with the museum's eight hour-a-day, seven days-a-week schedule?

I finally decided that a book containing recipes and menus might meet the needs of our guests. I asked the management of our museum store whether they thought such a book might be successful, and I was immediately assured that it would. I then asked various staff members if they thought a museum cookbook might be of value. Once again, I received an overwhelmingly positive response. Everyone liked the idea and was eager for its publication.

With the assistance of the museum's Curator, David Hanson and his able volunteers, I found an article in a 1945 issue of *Naval Institute Proceedings*, titled "Supplying The Fleet for 150 Years," by Commander J.W. Crumpacker (SC), U.S. Navy. The reading of this single article set my researcher's soul on fire, After that first article, a few hours turned into days spent alone at the back of our library rummaging through our collection of *Proceedings* articles until I had what was emerging to be much more than a mere recipe book. As is the dilemma of any researcher, I was faced with an essential question: Did I want to write a simple recipe book, as I had set out to do, or tell the story of food preparation throughout the history of our nation's navy?

Being an inveterate historian, I chose the latter. This history is the result of the journey I began among the yellowed pages of past issues of the *Naval Institute Proceedings*, the earliest article having been printed in 1906. I hope my reader enjoys the journey as much as I did.

While compiling the various recipes for each chapter, I realized that in many cases it was impossible for my readers to duplicate what was on the written page in their modern kitchens. That meant that I would have to find a means to modify and test a number of recipes. This was accomplished through the cooperation of the San Diego High School Culinary Arts Program, directed by Mrs. Linda Ross. Linda was kind enough to modify such recipes as "Spotted Dog" and "Sailor's Duff," and then have her students prepare them in their kitchen. This was followed by sampling and critique sessions with recommendations concerning how the recipes might be improved. The results of this process are published throughout the book and are written in *italics*.

On a final note, this collection is only representative of the total number of recipes available in the numerous resources I reviewed during my research. I have included only a small number of recipes from each era in order to give my reader a flavor of what our sailors were eating while living aboard their worlds afloat. I never intended for this recipe book to include all of the creations consumed by those who served our fleets at sea.

All times stated throughout the text are based on the 24-hour international time system.

ABOARD THE U.S.S. MIDWAY MUSEUM, BERTHED AT OLD NAVY PIER ON SAN DIEGO BAY, JUNE 21, 2007

Acknowledgements

Upon setting my course to write an expanded history of the evolution of the feeding of our nation's fleets, I had no idea of the myriad of resources I would call upon to compile this first of its kind publication. During my research I discovered a number of fine works describing the daily life of our sailors at sea. When I met dead-ends in my research, I was assisted in finding new tacks that led me to the discovery of my goals. As the sources for this work are as varied as are the ports of call made by any experienced sailor, I will note them below as they appear in the chapters of the work.

But before I begin our cruise I would like to thank some of those who have inspired as well as assisted my in this endeavor. I could not have set out on this journey without the assistance of my wonderful wife and editor, Louise. Her patience with me during the preparation of this collection is the single most important factor in its completion. I could not have begun this journey without the encouragement of my friend and mentor, Scott McGaugh, with whom I co-authored *Midway Memories* in 2006.

Some of my sources provided information on more than a single era of naval history. These were used in various chapters throughout the text. They include the Library of Congress, the Naval Historical Center, and the Military History Institute at Carlisle Barracks, Pennsylvania.

Individual issues of *U.S. Naval Institute Proceedings*, as well as works such as Nathan Miller's *U.S. Navy, An Illustrated History*, and *Picture History of the U.S. Navy*, by Theodore Roscoe and Fred Freeman were filled with information concerning early rations, food preparation equipment , and messing procedures.

Sources used for the writing of Chapter One include the excellent collections of recipes in *Lobscouse and Spotted Dog*, by Anne Chotzinoff Grossman and Lisa Grossman Thomas, and *The Illustrated Companion to Nelson's Navy*, by Nicholas Blake and Richard Lawrence. Patrick O'Brien's *Men-of War* was very useful in describing conditions below decks aboard British ships as well as the Standard British Seaman's Ration upon which a fledgling U.S. Navy based its ration during its early years. *The Anatomy of Nelson's Ships* by Nepean Longridge proved of great use in its illustrations of ships of the line and the location of their galleys and mess decks. Finally, the web site of the *U.S.S. Constitution* was my single source of a picture of a Cambouse Stove, commonly used aboard early American fighting ships.

Sources for chapter 2 concerning the Civil War were plentiful as was the assistance freely offered by web masters, curators, and re-enactors on the various web sites on the Internet. Of special use were *Civil War Interactive*, *Ironclads and Blockade Runners of the Civil War*, the *H.M.S. Warrior* web site, and *The Civil War Navies Message Board*. If my reader is interested in exploring these sites, he or she may simply Google the appropriate title(s) of interest. Published works include, but are not limited to *Life in Mr. Lincoln's Navy*, by Dennis J. Ringle, *The Civil War: The Coastal War*, by Peter M. Chaitin, and *A Taste for War*, by William C. Davis, both excellent resources for conditions afloat during this bloody war. Bruce Smith, curator of the Port Columbus Historical Site located at the Vicksburg National Military Park, was of special help in locating pictures of eating utensils used during this era.

Chapter 3 concerning the transition of food services after the Spanish-American War was written using many of the sources already cited, in particular articles published in *U.S. Naval Institute Proceedings* by Richard M. Anderson, Commander J. W. Crumpacher, Captain Norvelle W. Sharpe, Paymaster George P. Dyer, and Hanson W. Baldwin. Without the information contained in these articles, this narrative could not have been completed. Interspersed among the hours of drudgery spent by any researcher are moments when he or she stumbles upon a golden nugget of information that brings everything together and forms the heart of his work. Thus was my discovery of a copy of the U.S. Navy's first cookbook, published in 1902. *General Mess Manual and Cookbook for Use on Board Vessels of the United States Navy*, by The Paymaster General. This cook book was indeed a "golden nugget" of information.

Chapter 4 sources concerning food preparation were more difficult to locate than I thought would be the case. After many hours of futile searching, I finally located the web site, HyperWar: U.S. Navy in World War II, which contained a massive collection of bibliographical material that shed light on the complex solution of the massive logistics problems encountered by our country during this two-ocean war. *Ships Cook and Baker* and *Ship Stewards Handbook*, both by Otto Krey were useful sources of both recipes and procedures for food preparation and handling aboard our tanker, cargo and combination vessels during this era. Recipes used aboard our fighting ships were found in *The Cook Book of the United States Navy*, Bureau of Supplies and Accounts. The Navy training manual, *Instructions for the Use in Preparation for the Rating of Chief Commissary Steward*, 1940 edition, was filled with meal planning and preparation information.

The major resource for the recipes and conversion charts used in Chapter 5 are to be found in the Naval Logistics Library web site. Here my reader can read any one of some 1,689 recipes, plus information concerning the proper care and handling of a complete spectrum of food items served in our modern naval vessels as well as galleys ashore.

I would like to thank John "Mac" Mclaughlin, Rear Admiral, USN (Ret.), the President and CEO of the U.S.S. Midway Museum, for his continuing support and encouragement. I would also like to thank Sara Hanscom, Director of Educational Programs aboard the museum, as well as Midway Volunteers Mr. and Mrs. David Karle, who supported the program for the testing of a number of the recipes. Finally, I would like to give a personal "Bravo Zulu" to Mrs. Linda Ross and her students in the Culinary Arts Program at San Diego High School, for testing selected recipes as well as converting recipes developed to serve 100 or more hungry sailors to recipes for an equally hungry family of eight.

SAN DIEGO, CALIFORNIA, 2007

Chapter 1

FOODSTUFFS FOR AN EMERGING NAVY

*From The Revolutionary War
to war with the Barbary Pirates*

On August 9th, 1798, Captain Richard Dale of the newly established United States Navy stood quietly on one of the piers at the recently constructed naval yard in Portsmouth, New Hampshire. Behind him his crew loaded the frigate *U.S.S. Ganges* with rations prior to sailing. The waterfront was filled with excitement and noise as the crews of four newly outfitted frigates made ready for sea. Their mission was "to seize, take and bring into port of the United States, French armed ships committing depredations within one marine league of the coast between the Capes of Virginia and Long Island." Although the French had supported the colonies during their earlier struggle against the British, American merchant vessels were now being seized and sold as prizes by ships of both the French and British fleets.

Captain Dale's crew was taking aboard rations according to a list set down by the Congress of the United States in regulations establishing a permanent U.S. Navy in 1794. Section 8 of the two-page document read as follows:

"And be it further enacted, that the ration shall consist of as follows:

SUNDAY:	*1 lb bread, 1 ½ lb beef, ½ pt rice*
MONDAY:	*1 lb bread, 1 lb pork, ½ pt pease, 4 oz cheese*
TUESDAY:	*1 lb bread, 1 ½ lb beef, 1 lb potatoes or turnips and pudding*
WEDNESDAY:	*1 lb bread, 2 oz butter or, in lieu thereof, 6 oz molasses, 4 oz cheese and 1/2 pt rice*
THURSDAY:	*1 lb bread, 1 lb pork, ½ pint pease, ½ pt pease or beans*
FRIDAY:	*1 lb bread, 1 lb salt fish, 2 oz butter or 1 gill oil and 1 lb potatoes*
SATURDAY:	*1 lb bread, 1 lb pork, ½ pint pease or beans, 4 oz cheese."*

Congress also provided that "there shall also be allowed one-half pint of distilled spirits per day or, in lieu thereof, one quart of beer per day, to each daily ration." *(Reprinted from April 1952 All Hands Magazine)*

While the common seaman in 1798 was authorized a larger daily ration than his brothers-in-arms ashore, the quality of his fare had not improved much since the Revolutionary War. Sailors were traditional-minded fellows, and wanted their mess men to prepare dishes they were used to consuming. Although those serving in our nation's army might turn up their noses at some of the concoctions served in the fleet, the American sailor was content to stick to what he knew even though his rations often consisted of weevil-filled ship's biscuit and rancid "salt horse" made up into boiled duff puddings.

Only three-quarters of the cost of a day's ration in 1798 was delivered "in kind," meaning in the form of food, the other quarter being issued in currency to the leader of each individual enlisted mess. This currency, called commuted rations, was used to augment the food or "in kind" rations issued by the ship's purser, thus allowing the head of each mess to make purchases ashore or from bumboats of such things as herbs and spices, as well as unrefined sugar and vinegar. These additional purchases helped to liven up rations that could otherwise be quite tasteless. If a particular mess was fortunate enough to have a responsible leader, its members could look forward to some variety in their otherwise routine fare. If, on the other hand, the person responsible for management of the mess funds was less than reliable, he might gamble the funds away on a dog or horse race ashore, or even use the money to desert and fund his adventures ashore. In that case, his messmates would be limited to three-quarters rations from the very first day of the voyage.

Captain Dale and his fellow officers were by no means expected to consume the same fare as the rest of the crew. Officers in the Navy of 1798 were allocated rations according to their rank. Warrant Officers and Lieutenants received two rations per day while the commanding officers of frigates received a full six rations. However, this did not mean that commanding officers ate six times what the enlisted men ate. Captain Dale was expected to use the extra rations to feed the ship's boys who cleaned his cabin, prepared his food and served him. In addition, tradition dictated that he entertain his fellow officers and midshipmen from time to time, especially during long patrols at sea. Once the ship arrived at its assigned station he needed to have extra rations laid aside in case the need rose to entertain any guests who might be visiting aboard. As for the other officers, the extra rations covered the costs of feeding their servants. They were considered a form of payment in kind and could be sold back to the ship's purser for cash at the end of the voyage.

Another advantage to being an officer was that officers were allowed to draw their entire ration in cash (called a commuted ration). This allowed them to purchase their own provisions ashore instead of having to eat those issued by the ship's purser. (It was common practice to re-issue the unused rations of returning ships again and again until they were finally either consumed or found unfit for consumption by a ship's commanding officer.) Officers also augmented their food stocks by purchasing livestock such as pigs, cattle, and goats, as well as chickens and rabbits, thus adding fresh meat, milk and eggs to their daily ration until the stock was consumed. As if the shouts of Captain Dale's crew hoisting casks of salt horse and bags of ship's biscuits aboard were not enough, the sounds of lowing cattle and squealing pigs, the clucking of hens and the bleating of sheep added to the cacophony as the four ships made ready to put to sea on this August day.

After the last cask was stowed and the livestock made as comfortable as possible on the deck forward and under the poop deck aft, one half of the crew was allowed to go ashore for a last meal before setting sail the following morning. Eating ashore was quite a different thing for sailors. Knowing they would be confined to their ship for weeks or even months at a time, they were known to stuff themselves with lavish meals consisting of fresh oysters, beef, fish, and fowl liberally washed down with tankards of beer, ale and rum. Many of the crewmen drew advances on their pay from the ship's purser in order to partake in this final gastronomical orgy before putting out to sea. (Although the food has greatly improved in today's modern navy, officers and men alike flock to restaurants ashore to enjoy an escape from shipboard fare whenever the opportunity presents itself.)

Once the *U.S.S. Ganges* set sail, the crew quickly settled down into the routine of their watches. The sails having been set, the off watch went below while the other half of the crew set about making things shipshape for the long voyage ahead. Decks were cleaned, ropes and lines organized and stowed, and the first of many casks of "junk horse," (salted beef or pork) was lashed to the foremast. From this cask the ship's purser, or someone designated by Captain Dale, would soon issue the meat rations to the men. Before long, the rhythm of ship's work would become so routine that boredom became a major factor in the crew's lives aboard. Thus, any distractions were welcomed by all.

Meals were major events in the crew's daily routine. Not only did meals provide an opportunity to eat, but they also offered the crew an opportunity to sit and pass the time of day with their fellow crewmen as well as light up their pipes at the galley stove. Men aboard ship were divided into messes of eight men each. On a rotating basis throughout the week, one member of each mess served as mess cook for the day. Among those serving mess duty on the day the *U.S.S. Ganges* set sail was Able Seaman John Riplack, a member of the foretop watch mess. The men in this mess worked among the sails and rigging high above the ship's main deck and were considered to be the most able sailors in the crew.

NOTE THE LOCATION OF THE GALLEY STOVE, FORWARD ON THE MAIN DECK. ITS CHIMNEY IS CALLED THE "CHARLEY NOBEL"

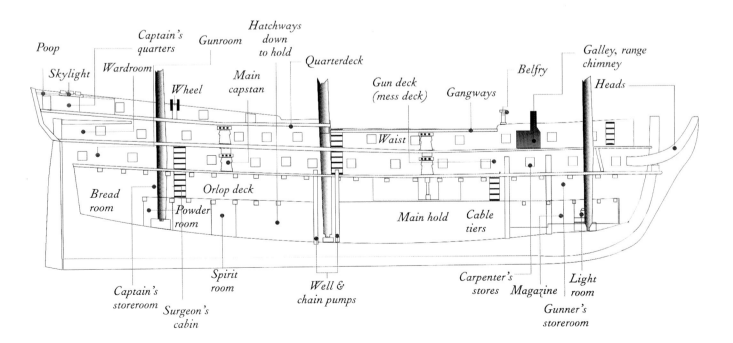

Promptly at 0900 the purser, a civilian, called for the mess men to collect the rations for the men in their individual mess. Riplack left his station aloft to go below to collect the salt horse ration for his mess in a small wooden bucket called a 'kid.' It being Tuesday, he also collected a pound of bread for each of his messmates, along with a pound of potatoes each. It was then left up to him to prepare the food and deliver his creation to the ship's cook, who was responsible for its cooking. Descending into the deck below the main deck where the sailors of the off watch stored their personal belongings and hung their hammocks when sleeping, John sought out his mess' food chest. This small wooden box was used for storing the utensils shared by the members of the mess, items purchased to augment the provisions supplied by the ship, and food left over from a meal for consumption later. Being an experienced sailor, he had used his mess' commuted rations wisely, purchasing small amounts of seasonings ashore such as cinnamon, ginger, baking soda and the like to enhance his creations while at sea. It was not long before John had mixed up a Dandyfunk, (See the recipe he used on page 17.) which he wrapped securely in a canvas bag for cooking. He placed the potatoes in another canvas bag and secured it tightly so none of them would be lost in the pot of boiling water into which they would be placed for cooking. After placing the bread ration and the unused spices back into the chest, he returned the food chest to its place against the starboard bulkhead and made ready to deliver his creation to the galley.

Proceeding forward, John took his place in the queue of fellow mess men awaiting their turns at the steaming cauldrons presided over by the ship's cook. These large copper pots filled with boiling water, sat atop a massive cast iron stove set in sand on the ship's deck. Fueled by either wood or coal, the smoke of which was vented through a stovepipe called the "Charlie Noble," this massive stove served both the enlisted and officers' messes.

Upon reaching the head of the line, John presented his "duff" to the cook who attached a wooden identifying tag to it. The "pudding" was then lowered into boiling water. Some puddings such as those containing pork and peas were tied tightly to prevent their becoming diluted in the boiling water, while others containing flour were packed loosely in their open-topped cotton containers so they could expand during cooking. The cook attached another wooden tag to the bag of small potatoes John presented him and hung the bag from a pole extending across the steaming mouth of the kettle. His work done for the present, John then scrambled back up the ratlines to resume his work far above the ship's rolling deck.

At 1130 hours, John was piped down from his workstation aloft to return to the galley to pick up his rations and carry them to the place where his

STORAGE OF WATER, RUM, AND DRY STORES ABOARD A TWO-MASTED SCHOONER.

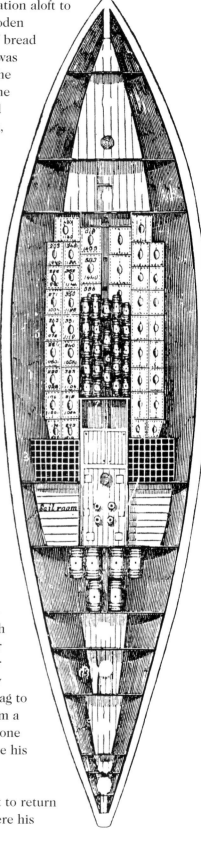

mess would eat. Before getting the hot food from the galley, John went below to the crew berthing area and picked up the mess' wooden mess chest and the mess kid, a wooden vessel with rope handles used to carry the hot food from the galley to where the men in his mess would take their meal. Emerging onto the main deck, he placed the mess chest at the foot of the main mast. He then took a square of canvas out of the box and spread it on the deck. On this he placed small packets of salt and pepper and a container of vinegar. He then picked up the mess kid and went to the galley to reclaim his bags of now thoroughly boiled food. After returning to his mess area at the foot of the mast, he turned the pudding out of its container and placed it on a square of canvas. He then cut the pudding into eight pieces with the same clasp knife he had been using just moments before to cut tarred lines aloft. He then deposited the cut up Dandyfunk back into the center of the messkid. Opening the bag of boiled potatoes, he arranged them carefully around the pudding. He then placed a small piece of canvas over the whole lot so it would be warm when the crew was called to dinner.

ONE SIDE OF THE GALLEY STOVE WAS USED FOR ROASTING THE OFFICERS' FRESH MEAT, THE OTHER FOR BOILING THE CREW'S PUDDINGS.

The crew was piped to dinner promptly at 1200. After everyone had taken his place on the deck around the "kid," John uncovered the wooden container, exposing the pudding and potatoes to the other members of the mess. Topman Fenton, the senior member of the mess, opened his clasp knife and speared the largest of the potatoes and the best looking piece of the pudding. Placing them on his portion of the canvas John had stretched at the foot of the mast, he then set to eating while the other members of the mess speared potatoes and pudding for themselves. Although the ship's purser offered forks and spoons for sale at a low price, most sailors found it more convenient to spear the pieces of hard pudding with their personal clasp knife rather than going below to rummage through their personal kit to retrieve their eating utensils. A sailor arriving late at the mess was going to come up short as it was every man for himself after the senior member of the mess had taken his portion. Square wooden trenchards, (a possible source of the term "a square meal."), and bowls were also offered for sale to the crew, but few men used them except when thick stews or soups were served.

SET IN A BED OF SAND OR ON BRICKS, THE STOVE WAS FIRED BY COAL. NOTE THE TWO BOILING POTS FOR COOKING A CREW'S MEAL.

After the crew had eaten their fill, John cleaned up the condiments and the 'kid' and stowed that portion of the ration not consumed by his messmates in the mess chest for the evening meal and the next morning's breakfast. He then scraped any remaining "pudding" from the canvas cloth with the blade of his knife, licked the blade clean, and returned the cloth to the chest. After stowing the mess box and messkid below on the berth deck, John joined his messmates among the jungle of lines at the foretop mast. This midday meal known as dinner was the only hot meal prepared for the crew each day. For supper, which was usually served at 1700, and breakfast, which was served at 0700 the next morning, the men were expected to subsist on leftovers, ship's biscuit, coffee or tea, and whatever John had purchased ashore with the commuted portion of the mess' ration.

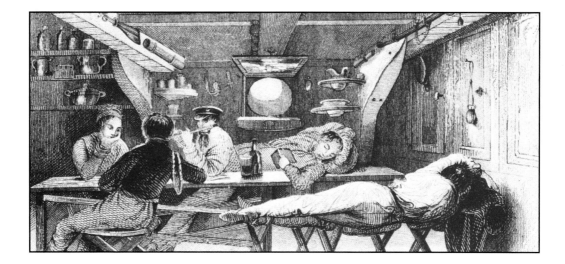

WARRANT OFFICERS

HAD A PRIVATE

MESS WHERE THEY

BOTH ATE AND SLEPT.

While the crew ate on the deck above, two stewards who had retrieved the officers' food from the cook stove forward and three ship's boys prepared and served meals to Captain Dale and his fellow officers below. In the case of the *Ganges,* there was not a space large enough for all of the officers to dine together. Of course the captain was provided with a cabin, but the rest of the officers were left to their own devices to find a place to eat their meals. As officers' cabins were nothing more than small cells, usually shared by two or three men, the *Ganges'* officers took their meals, served by the ship's boys on pewter or wooden bowls or trays the officers had purchased themselves. Balancing their food against the roll of the vessel, the officers then went to the wardrobe where they stored their sea trunks. Sitting on their trunks arrayed about the deck, the officers balanced their bowls or plates wherever they might and ate their meals using personal eating utensils which included knives, forks and spoons as well as tankards or mugs. Thus was born the wardroom, which is the space where today's naval officers dine while aboard ship.

Some recipes still survive from those early navy days. Among those surviving recipes I am including such tasty concoctions as Dandyfunk, as prepared by Able Seaman Riplack, Duff, Spotted Dog, and Sea Pie. Also included is a recipe for ship's biscuit, a staple found in many recipes of the day. Notice that in many of the original recipes there are no quantities given for individual ingredients. Mess men were expected to use what was available and season their recipes to their individual tastes. I have been careful to copy the recipes exactly as I found them, being true to abbreviations and punctuation used at the time.

A MESS EATING

DINNER ON THE

SHIP'S DECK.

Selected recipes were tested in the kitchens of the Culinary Arts Center at San Diego High School in San Diego, California. There, students cooked the recipes as written, noted their reactions to the taste and texture of the final products, and made recommendations concerning how the recipes might be improved.

SHIP'S BISCUIT

(This is the original version of this staple of the seaman's diet.)
Students in the Culinary Arts Program at San Diego High School tested this recipe. They universally agreed that the results were tasteless and difficult to chew. They did, however find that the biscuits were easy to store and beat into powder for subsequent use in other recipes.

Ingredients:

– 3 1/2 cups whole wheat flour
– Salt to taste
– 1 1/2 cups water

Instructions:

– Mix salt and whole wheat flour and enough water to form a very stiff dough.
– Roll the dough to a thickness of 3/4 - 1 inch.
– Cut into 3 inch squares and punch liberally with holes using a medium-sized nail or a carving fork.
– Bake in a flat pan at 250 degrees F. for 2 or 3 hours.

DANDYFUNK

(This was a sailor's favorite meal)

Instructions:

– Soak six navy biscuits per serving (see recipe above) in water.
– Mash with a pestle or marlinspike, (a sharply-pointed iron pin used by sailors to splice line)
– Mix with the fat taken from the coppers where the meat is boiled.
– Flavor with allspice, if available
– Wrap tightly in a pudding cloth and boil for two hours until cooked through
– Slice for serving
– Sweeten with molasses, if available

Note: I have also found a recipe where the ingredients are placed in a pan and covered with molasses, then baked until done.

SALT JUNK AND SHIP'S BISCUIT

Instructions:

– Pound some ship's biscuits per man into a powder
– Add cut-up salt pork or beef that has been soaked overnight *(I found one recipe where salt cod was substituted for the salted meat. In this case, the fish was soaked overnight as was the meat.)*
– Tie tightly in a pudding cloth
– Boil for two hours
– Serve by cutting pudding into rounds

Note: In this case, no quantity is given for either the ship's biscuit or the salt pork or beef. Mess men were supposed to have learned the quantities necessary through experience and the guidance of their more experienced mess mates.

SAILOR'S DUFF

(Similar to gingerbread, this modern version of the basic seaman's recipe is best served warm.)

Ingredients:

- 1/2 cup brown sugar, packed firmly
- 2 tablespoons butter
- 1/8 teaspoon baking soda
- 2 tablespoons dark molasses
- 1 teaspoon cinnamon
- 1/2 teaspoon powdered ginger
- 1 egg
- 1/2 cup milk
- 1 teaspoon baking powder
- 1 cup un-sifted all-purpose flour

Instructions:

- Cream together brown sugar and butter. Dissolve baking soda in molasses and add to brown sugar mixture; mix well. Add cinnamon, ginger, egg, milk, baking powder and flour. Pour into a battered pudding mold or buttered 1-pound coffee can.

- To steam, set on a rack in a large deep kettle, add boiling water to come halfway up the sides of the mold or coffee can. Bring water to a gentle boil, cover the kettle, lower heat and steam for 1 1/2 hours. Serve warm with sauce.

San Diego High School students modified the cooking instructions to accommodate the modern kitchen:

- Place pudding mold into a water bath.
- Bake in a 350 oven for about 1 1/2 hour until set.
- Serve warm with sauce

SAILOR'S DUFF SAUCE

Ingredients:

- 2 egg yolks
- 1/2 cup granulated sugar
- 2 tablespoons brandy
- 1 cup heavy cream

Instructions:

- Beat egg yolks well, gradually adding sugar. Add brandy and blend. Just before serving, whip cream and fold into sauce.

BURGOO

This early version of our more modern cooked oatmeal served sailors as a hearty meal to begin their day when they could talk the ship's cook into lighting the cook stove on a cold, rainy day at sea. (Serves 4)

Ingredients:

- 2 cups steel-cut oats
- 4 cups water
- 1 tsp. salt
- 3 tablespoons butter
- 4 teaspoons sugar

Instructions:

- Gradually stir oats into water.
- Set over medium heat to boil.
- Reduce heat and simmer for 15 minutes, stirring constantly.
- Remove from heat, add remaining ingredients, stir to dissolve.

OFFICERS' FARE

The ship's officers had boys to assist the cook in the preparation of their meals, thus the recipes tended to be far more complex than those prepared by the crew. This meant that the preparation of many of the officer's dishes required the cook to do more than boil them in the ship's pots. The recipes that follow were favorites of both the wardroom and the captain's table during the 18th century.

SEA PIE

(This Sea Pie has only a single level of filling. Some recipes have a number of layers of various meats and gravies separated from one another by layers of pastry.)

Ingredients:

– Three large onions cut into rounds

– 1 pound pork or beef cut into small pieces

– Two potatoes cut in quarters

– 2 tablespoons butter

– 2 tablespoons flour mixed with enough water to produce a gravy

– Salt

– Pepper

– Dough sufficient to cover sides and top of baking pan
  (see recipe on the following page for Sea Pie Dough)

Instructions:

– Simmer together onions, fried brown, lean meat cut into small pieces, and potatoes cut into quarters.

– Prepare dough and cover the sides of a baking pan.

– Mix flour and water together and pour over simmering ingredients.

– When thickened, pour stew into lined baking pan.

– Season with salt and pepper.

– Cover pan with thick crust.

– Bake for two hours.

Note: When we tested this recipe, we added about a half cup of tomato catsup to the stew before we added it to the baking pan. We found it to be a definite improvement!

SEA PIE DOUGH

(This makes enough dough for a large enough Sea Pie to feed the entire wardroom, so you may want to scale back the quantities if you are feeding a small number of guests.)

Ingredients:

– 2 cups water

– 1/2 pound butter

– 1/2 pound lard or suet

– 9 cups flour

– 1 tablespoon salt

Instructions:

– Warm water, butter and lard or suet* together over moderate heat until all are liquid.

– In large trenchard or bowl combine flour and salt, then add the hot liquid and mix thoroughly.

– Turn the dough out onto a lightly floured board and knead for about 5 minutes.

– Place the dough in a container, cover with a cloth, and let rest in a warm place for about 30 minutes.

Suet is the fat from around the loin or kidney of mutton or beef. When used, it is chopped finely before adding to the other ingredients.

"SPOTTED DOG"

(This is the basic recipe used by both sailors and officers during the 18th Century. Note the lack of any quantities in this recipe.)

Instructions:

– Mix flour, lard or grated pork fat, raisins, saleratus (baking soda), and eggs (if available)

– Place in canvas bag, wide at the top and narrow at the bottom, and boil for two hours.

– Serve on a platter with wine sauce

Wine sauce substitute

– Boil together vinegar, butter, sugar, and water.

– Thicken with flour and flavor with nutmeg

DROWNED (BOILED) BABY

Ingredients:

– 4 cups flour

– 1/4 cup sugar

– 1/2 teaspoon salt

– 1 teaspoon ground cinnamon

– 1 1/2 cups raisins

– 1/2 pound suet, finely grated

– Ice water

Instructions:

– Mix the dry ingredients together in a large bowl. Stir in the raisins, breaking them apart (the flour will coat them and keep them from clumping together. Mix in the suet.

– Work in 1 - 2 tablespoons ice water. Continue gradually adding ice water until a stiff paste is formed (it may take as much as a cup of ice water). Work it until it forms a ball. Turn it out onto a well-floured board. Cover with a damp cloth and let rest for 15 minutes.

– Knead the dough until it is shiny and elastic (6-8 minutes), cover again and let rest for another 5 minutes, then knead again for 1-2 minutes.

– Shape the dough into a short, cylindrical lump. Wrap the pudding loosely in a well-floured piece of cotton cloth. Tie securely at both ends, wrapping one end of the string loosely around the covering from one end-knot to the other to keep the cloth from gaping open in the middle. Immerse the pudding in a pot of boiling water and cook for 2 1/2 hours, replenishing the water as necessary.

– To serve, untie and unroll the pudding from its cloth container. Turn the pudding out onto a serving platter. Serve hot, best accompanied by a custard sauce. Serves 12 - 16

LOBSCOUSE

(This recipe for a fragrant stew of meats, potatoes and ship's biscuit finds its origins in maritime history long lost to historians. Its complexity reflects 18th century wardroom cooking at its best.)

Students testing this recipe used fresh beef and pork. They also left out the juniper berries. They found their final product to be a hearty stew, both fragrant and satisfying in texture.

Ingredients:

- 2 pounds salt beef, soaked 24 hours in fresh water. After 24 hours the water is poured off and the beef rinsed in fresh water.
- 2 pounds salt pork treated the same as the salt beef
- 4 large onions
- 6 large potatoes
- 8 ounces Ship's Biscuit
- 6 juniper berries, crushed
- 1 teaspoon allspice
- 1 teaspoon ground nutmeg
- 1 teaspoon mace
- 1/2 teaspoon ground cloves
- 1/2 teaspoon ground cardamom
- Ground pepper to taste

Instructions:

- Put beef and pork in cold water to cover and bring to a boil over medium heat until tender (about 3 hours) *Because our student cooks used fresh beef and pork, this cooking time was greatly reduced.*
- Remove from heat, skim and reserve any fat.
- Reserve 3 cups of cooking liquid.
- Trim the meats and dice into 1/4-inch cubes.
- Peel onions and potatoes and cut into 1/4 inch cubes.
- Pound Ship's Biscuit into course crumbs with a marlinspike. *(Students used a metal rolling pin. You can use 8 ounces of whole wheat flour)*
  - Heat six tablespoons of the fat reserved from the boiling meat in a frying pan over high heat.
  - Add the meats and brown (10 to 12 minutes).
  - Remove the meat from the pan reserving as much of the fat as possible.
  - Sauté the onions over medium heat in same pan, adding a bit more of the reserved fat if needed, until they begin to brown. Add the potatoes to the onions and cook, stirring often for about 5 or 6 minutes.
    - Add the browned meat, cover and cook for 5-10 minutes over medium-low heat until the potatoes are tender-crisp.
      - Stir in the pounded biscuit and 1 1/2 cups of the reserved liquid (more if you like your stew thinner). Add the spices and pepper to taste.
        - Mix well. Cover and cook another 5 minutes, then serve.

BOILED PEASE 'N PORK

Instructions:

- Mash 1/2 pint of peas per man in a piece of sailcloth, pounding them with a marlin spike
- Add 1/2 pound pork that has been soaked overnight, cut into small pieces
- Mix thoroughly and tie tightly in a pudding bag with an extra tie amidships of the bag
- Deliver to the cook for boiling for two to three hours until done.
- Cut the ties and roll out the pudding onto a clean cloth.
- Cut and serve

DOG'S BODY, OR PEASE-PUDDING

(This recipe serves 8 as a side dish.)

Ingredients:

- 1 lb. dried split pease
- 6 oz. salt pork, cut into 1/2 inch dice
- 4 tablespoons flour or pounded ship's biscuit
- 1 teaspoon salt
- Pepper to taste

Instructions:

- Tie the pease loosely in a piece of sailcloth or pudding cloth.
- Place in a large pot of boiling water to cover being sure the cloth does not touch the bottom of the pot.
- Simmer, covered for 1 1/2 hours.
- Place in a mess kid and let cool.
- When cool enough to handle, squeeze out as much liquid as possible.
- Open the bag and scrape out the peas into the mess kid.
- Add the salt pork, flour and spices and mix well.
- Put the mixture back into the cloth and place the pudding in a fresh pot of boiling water.
- Cook for 1 hour.
- Turn pudding out into kid and serve.

FLIP

While the crew was limited to their daily ration of beer or grog, the ship's officers enjoyed a number of alcoholic concoctions similar to today's mixed drinks.

Ingredients:

- 1 egg
- 1 pint dry sherry
- 1/2 teaspoon ground nutmeg
- 2 teaspoons sugar
- 1 teaspoon butter

Instructions:

- Have two large earthenware jugs close at hand.
- In one jug, beat together the egg and one teaspoon dry sherry.
- Heat the remaining dry sherry, nutmeg, sugar and butter until almost boiling.
- Gradually add the hot mixture to the egg mixture stirring rapidly to keep the egg from curdling.
- Now pour the mixture back and forth between the two earthenware jugs until it becomes frothy.
- Enjoy.

ORANGE SHRUB

Instructions:

– Break one hundred pounds of loaf sugar in small pieces, boil until the sugar is melted, skim it well, and put it into a tub to cool; when cold, put it on a cask, with thirty gallons of good Jamaica rum, and fifteen gallons of orange juice, (mind to strain all the seeds out of the juice) and mix them well together; then beat up the whites of six eggs very well, stir them well in, let it stand a week to fine, then draw off for use.

Note: Spirits and beer played an important role in the early navy. Not only did they make the water carried aboard naval vessels more palatable, they were also said to have a calming effect upon the crew. Issued twice a day, a quarter of a pint at a time, this part of the ration was considered the only luxury the crew had while aboard ship. Captains sometimes gave their crews extra rations of grog either before an action to help shore up their courage, or after a victory as a reward for a job well done.

Admiral Vernon of the Royal Navy was the originator of grog in 1740. During a cruise in the West Indies he had local rum diluted in water issued to his victorious crew. Since he was known as "Old Grog" because of the long cloak made of grogram he wore, his men named the drink after him. Since that day, the drink of one part rum and two parts water has been known as grog.

After the Revolutionary War, farmers requested that the Congress of our new nation replace the imported rum ration with whiskey which was produced locally. The Navy Department complied, and in 1806 issued new regulations stating whiskey was to replace the rum ration because of its being "a more wholesome drink."

The ration was reduced to one gill, (1/4 pint) or half a pint of wine in 1842 by then Secretary of the Navy John Branch. The ration was limited to men over the age of twenty-one, those of lower age receiving instead an allowance of three to five cents a day.

Officers generally maintained a wide variety of wines and brandies which were consumed on a daily basis either during meals or while off watch. Mixed drinks were common, varying from simple combinations of alcoholic spirits and water to complex recipes containing as many as eight or even ten individual ingredients. Supplies of both grog and the officers' wine and spirits were kept locked securely in a special hold located near the officers' quarters. If the ship was large enough to warrant a Marine detachment, a Marine guard was posted at the entryway to this compartment.

Chapter 2

NAVY TACK, NORTH AND SOUTH
Victualing the Union and Confederate Navies

SIXTY-FIVE YEARS AFTER CAPTAIN RICHARD DALE stood watching his crew prepare *Ganges* for sea on the pier at the newly constructed Naval Yards at Portsmouth, New Hampshire, another naval officer stood proudly contemplating the morning activity of the crew loading supplies aboard his newly commissioned ship. Captain John Rodgers and a crew of seventy-four officers and men had commissioned the *U.S.S. Weehawken*, a 1,875-ton Passaic class monitor built at Jersey City, New Jersey on January 16, 1863. After conducting sea trials in the Atlantic Ocean, Captain Rodgers had been ordered to take on supplies at Portsmouth in preparation for steaming south to join the Southern Squadron off Port Royal, South Carolina. There, he would join in the blockading of the southern coastline in order to stop supplies from getting to the Confederacy by sea.

The United States was once again at war, this time against the thirteen southern states that had seceded from the Union two years earlier. The states that now made up the Union had been flexing their manufacturing muscles by building a new class of ship, the Monitor. The nature of seafaring vessels had changed greatly. The steam engine had been invented, and a modified version adapted for shipboard use. By 1863, steam-powered, propeller-driven vessels were as common a sight on the waters of the North American continent as sailing vessels had been only fifty years before. And now those steam engines were mounted in ships constructed completely of thick steel plates, riveted or bolted together to protect their crews from enemy fire.

The *Weehawken* had a length of 200 feet and a beam of 46 feet. Although she had a draft of 10 and a-half feet, her heavy weight caused her bow to ride only four feet above the placid waters of the Piscataquis River. During her sea trials, her bow had spent more time under the surface of the oncoming sea than above it. Although she could be out-sailed by nearly any of the older sailing ships anchored in the harbor, the ship's 5-knot speed was sufficient to lay her alongside her enemies hiding in bays and inlets along the southern coastline in order to bring her two Dahlgren smoothbore cannons to bear (One had a 15 inch bore, the other an 11 inch). Both of these heavy guns were mounted in a revolving turret mounted amidships.

NAVAL SUPPLIES
BEING READIED
FOR LOADING
ABOARD A
BLOCKADING SHIP.

Captain Rodgers was shaken from his thoughts by the sound of a box of provisions smashing against the steel deck behind him. The subsequent curses by the two sailors who had been attempting to pass the box of canned goods through the small door in the turret was stilled by a shout from the Ship's Cook who was overseeing the loading of provisions. After setting the men to picking up the cans and passing them below, the line of provisions once again began to disappear into the ship. A similar line of men, supervised by the ship's Commissary Officer, was busy passing provisions through a small deckhouse forward.

On July 18, 1861, Congress had approved a daily ration for the Navy that incorporated a much broader selection of nutritious foods and vegetables than that ordered in 1794:

One pound salt pork, with half a pint of beans or peas; or one pound salt beef, with half a pound of flour, and two ounces of dried apples or other fruit; or three quarters of preserved meat (canned), with half a pound of rice, two ounces of butter, and one ounce of desiccated mixed vegetables; or three quarters pound preserved meat, two ounces of butter, and two ounces of desiccated potato; together with fourteen ounces of biscuits (hardtack), one quarter of an ounce of tea, or one ounce of coffee or cocoa, two ounces of sugar, and a gill (four ounces) of spirits (grog); and a weekly allowance of a half a pound of pickles, half a pint of molasses, and half a pint of vinegar.

This allowance exceeded the Army's rations by four ounces of salt pork, one-half ounce of desiccated potatoes, and a half-ounce of coffee. The Navy also supplied its

THE UNION NAVY'S
BLOCKADE OF THE
CONFEDERATE
COASTLINE.

crews with butter packed in small containers called firkins, while Army troops received no such ration. One quarter of the daily ration continued to be issued to the individual messes in cash. This enabled the messes to augment their government issued staples with a variety of items purchased ashore or from civilian craft.

Two important technological innovations helped to make this new ration more palatable for the Union sailors. First, the canning of meats had been invented in England as early as 1804, but had not been used on a grand scale by the U.S. Navy until 1860 when Gilbert Van Camp Company introduced canned pork and beans packed in tomato sauce. By 1863, the U.S. Navy was purchasing canned meats in tins weighing from 2 to 6 pounds. This important technical advance allowed the Navy to provide its sailors with a varied diet that was packed in containers that could withstand the rigors of a sea passage.

A second innovation was the ability to process foods, removing a majority of the moisture from fruits and vegetables through the application of hydraulic pressure. Known as "desiccated vegetables," these items could be reconstituted by soaking them in water when needed, thus allowing ships to be stocked with such items as onions, carrots, turnips, potatoes, apricots and apples without having to worry about spoilage.

Although the food was greatly improved, Captain Rodgers' crew still depended heavily on salt horse and ship's biscuit for their meals. Ship's biscuit had grown in size a bit from that provided the early navy, but it was still produced using the same ingredients and process as before. The biscuit was still plagued by mold, maggots, and weevils, but Civil War era sailors were hardy fellows and continued to consume the crackers, worms and all. One sailor wrote: "Break open a hardtack and perhaps two or three worms would lie embedded in the - well, cracker. But after being on board some time I could munch them equal to any vet, without examining the interior."

Another thing that had changed with time was the position of ship's cook. The civilian purser had been replaced by a commissioned officer who was assigned the duties of managing the ship's stores. The cook was directly responsible to this officer and in many cases acted as his agent in the distribution and preparation of the crew's rations. Thus, on this day in 1863, Ship's Cook Daniel Jacobs, formerly employed by a well-known hotel in New York City, found himself quite busy while he and the ship's Commissary Officer, Lieutenant Robert St. James, checked each item against the ration inventory as they stood guard at the two entry portals while the crew passed containers of desiccated vegetables aboard for storage below.

Ship's Cook was the first official non-commissioned or warrant rating in the U.S. Navy. Unlike the Army, where every man was left to his own devices to prepare his meals, the Department of the Navy had seen fit to assign a number of men to its ships with the express duty of food preparation. In many cases these men had worked in restaurants or inns prior to volunteering for naval service. The skills Daniel Jacobs brought aboard after learning his trade in one of New York's premium hotels would make the crew the envy of many of the other ships in the Southern Squadron. Not only would her crew eat well, but the wardroom of the *Weehawken* was to become quite popular with the senior officers of the squadron who were invited aboard to dine with the captain from time to time.

In addition to the inventorying and issuing of rations to the various messes aboard, Ship's Cook Jacobs also supervised three assistant cooks who aided the mess cooks in the preparation of meals. Although some things had changed, the breaking up of the enlisted crew into messes of from 8 to 15 men, usually from the same rating or watch rotation, was much like it had been before the Revolutionary War.

Mess cooks were still assigned the duties of drawing their mess' rations, and then delivering the prepared portion of that ration to the galley where the cooks cooked it. Each mess cook then went to his mess' common chest where he took out each member's cup and tin plate of "agateware" (tin coated with a baked-on enamel coating resembling marbled stone), knife, fork and spoon, setting them out in an orderly fashion upon a piece of canvas spread on the deck. Next, he laid out the appropriate condiments such as salt and pepper, vinegar, or syrup for the use of his mess mates.

The mess cook then deposited the ration of either soft bread (if the ship's cooks had found the time to bake such the day before), or Ship's Biscuit alongside the utensils. Next he drew a bucket of boiling water into which he deposited the beverage of the day which could be coffee, tea, or some concoction purchased when last ashore. After stirring the mixture, he covered the pot and left it to steep.

When the men were piped to eat, the mess cook would ladle out the beverage to each man in the mess, then go to the galley to pick up the hot meal prepared by the cooks. This he carried to the gathered members of his mess in one or two pots, according to the menu, cut it up into equal portions, then served it out. After everyone had been served, he proceeded to eat his portion of the meal.

After the meal was consumed, the mess cook cleaned up the area, drew water from the galley, and washed the utensils and the mess area, returning the utensils to the common chest along with any left over condiments. He then folded and put away the canvas. If the mess cook volunteered to assume the duties of food preparation for longer than one day, he was provided with a small monetary stipend from the other members of his mess.

The addition of a hot meal served for breakfast sometimes taxed the creativeness of the ship's mess cooks. A day's meals is described by one crewman aboard a cruiser in the Southern Squadron:

> *We go down to breakfast which consists of a pan of potato scouse (potatoes and hardtack cooked together with butter and any herbs the mess cook may have in his mess chest), a pot of hot coffee (boiling water was always available aboard these steam-driven vessels), and plenty of hard bread (hardtack). At noon we have dinner consisting of fresh bread and vegetable soup with beef (prepared by mixing desiccated vegetables which had to be reconstituted by soaking in fresh water, with salted beef which had to be soaked in fresh water for at least 12 hours to remove the salt in which it had been preserved). At 4PM we get supper, which consists of cold leftovers, hot tea or coffee and hard bread.*

The Monitors were notoriously hot. The ships only had a single deck with an overhead sometimes as low as four or five feet. Steam lines ran from the boilers to the steam engines making the area below deck hot and humid. The addition of the heat generated by a galley stove to this environment sometimes stretched the endurance of the crew. Each monitor was thus issued a small, portable stove for cooking on deck in fair weather.

Fresh meat and vegetables turned bad quickly in the heat below decks, making it necessary to move food storage to the cooler main deck. The captain of the *Nahant*, another Passaic class monitor in the squadron, had an ice chest installed on the main deck of his ship aft of the pilothouse. This proved to be an effective way to preserve the freshness of meats and vegetables delivered bi-weekly by the supply ships, and soon other ships of the squadron were using this innovation.

Even with the re-supply system the U.S. Navy had in place to support the ships on blockade duty, ships often ran out of fresh provisions. In these cases, the crew resorted to the age-old recipes using salt horse and

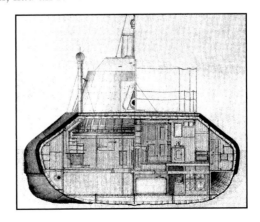

THE SHIP'S STOVE WAS LOCATED DIRECTLY BELOW AND TO STARBOARD OF THE MONITOR'S FORWARD TURRET.

mixtures of flour, ground peas and beans and ship's biscuit. During a period of five months, the crew of the *U.S.S. Hartford* was forced to eat canned pork and beans for dinner 34 percent of the time. On several instances, crewmen of ships operating close inshore held hunting parties to supply their crews with fresh meat.

There was another large fleet of ships fighting the war in the heartland of the nation as U.S. forces attempted to cut the Confederacy in half by controlling the vast length of the Mississippi River. This "fresh water navy" was supplied from ports in the north such as Saint Louis and the Union's main supply base in the west located in Cairo, Illinois. Connected to supply points by flat-bottomed river boats purchased from civilian steamship companies, these forces had fewer problems with supply than did their brothers who served in the blockading navy at sea. Traveling along the nation's rivers and tributaries in water sometimes as shallow as three feet, these ships sent hunting parties ashore to harvest rabbits, turkeys, and squirrels, all of which provided welcome respite from the desiccated vegetables and pork and beans provided to them by the government.

Fresh meat and vegetables found their way to crews of patrolling craft as well as smoked hams and bacon produced by loyal farmers along the inland waterways.

Union Officers continued to draw commuted rations, or cash, in lieu of food and spirit rations. Command and flag officers had their own messes, while officers of the rank of lieutenant and below ate together in the wardroom, which by now had evolved into a formal dining room. The ship's cook prepared the officers' meals separately from the crew's, while stewards and ship's boys still assisted in the preparation and serving of officers' meals. Officers ate together at a long table using porcelain plates, and in many cases, silver utensils. They maintained extensive supplies of both wines and spirits and continued to consume sometimes vast quantities of both when off duty.

Crews of Confederate vessels did not fare as well as those in the U.S. Navy. The Confederate Navy based its ration upon that adopted by the United States Navy in 1842; a ration still emphasizing salt pork or beef, rice and dried peas or beans. While fresh vegetables were supplied in port, scarcity of food was always a serious problem within the Confederacy.

Midshipman James Morris Morgan onboard the Confederate School Ship *C.S.S. Patrick Henry* in late 1864 summed up the rations of the day ashore:

> *The menu offered little variety. If it was not a tiny lump of fat pork, it was a shaving of fresh meat as tough as the hide which had once covered it, with a piece of hardtack and a tin cup of hot water colored by chicory or grains of burned corn, ground up, and brevetted coffee. But no one kicked about the food, as it was as good if not better than that the poor soldiers in the trenches received.*

Confederate naval vessels serving inshore as protection for the various coastal forts or ports sent parties ashore to hunt and trade for fresh provisions to augment their meager shipboard fare.

 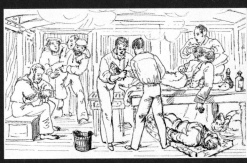

THE WARDROOM ABOARD A MONITOR WAS HOT AND CRAMPED. DURING BATTLE, IT SERVED AS A SURGERY FOR THE WOUNDED.

Some relief from these shortages was gained aboard the numerous Confederate cruisers that preyed upon northern vessels. While items such as cheese, butter, raisins, coffee and tea were never available when ashore, they could suddenly become available when a raider stopped a Union merchantman heading for a northern port. John McIntosh Kell, the executive officer of the *Alabama*, wrote that his men "lived almost entirely on our prizes." When these cruisers returned to their southern ports they would sometimes offload massive quantities of stores taken from Union prizes. The naval authorities would immediately dispatch these stores to other vessels in the area.

The sailors of both navies continued to prefer their daily issues of grog to the more readily available rations of coffee and tea. One sailor gave an excellent description of the method used in distributing the daily ration:

> *Grog was served out twice a day, in the morning before breakfast and again at night before piping down for supper. When the Boatswain piped for grog time, the crew fell into line and marched in single file, before the ship's steward, who dealt out each share as he came up. Each man received one gill (four ounces) in a small round measure...a master-at-arms and a marine stood by to see that each man got his ration and that no man was served twice.*

THE CREW RECEIVED ITS SPIRIT RATION, SERVED TWICE A DAY, UNDER THE WATCHFUL EYE OF A SHIP'S OFFICER.

Although several of the more conservative members of the U.S. Congress lobbied for the ending of the grog ration as early as 1841, Southern congressmen voted the attempts down. In 1862, the Southern lobby was broken because the dissenters no longer shared the halls of Congress with the more conservative representatives of the North. To the dismay of the sailors, a new ration law was passed and the grog ration was ended on 1 September 1862.

Officers were still allowed to maintain a wine mess, but strong spirits had at last departed from the standard navy ration.

Recipes from this era reflect the improvements in the construction of galley stoves, methods of food preservation, and advances in the field of medicine. Although a few recipes for boiled puddings still existed, more dishes called for baking and roasting. An increased number of vegetables were included in dishes and fruit played a greater role in the diet. Naval forces able to trade with run-away slaves, or northern sympathizers, or able to hunt and fish along the coast line could augment their menus with fresh eggs, corn, apples, grapes, chickens and pigs. While ashore, the ship's cooks as well as mess cooks were expected to purchase herbs to be used as seasoning in addition to salt and pepper.

THE UNION NAVY ATTRACTED RECRUITS WITH OFFERS OF PRIZE MONEY FOR CAPTURED CONFEDERATE SHIPS. NO MENTION WAS MADE OF THE MONTHS OF BOREDOM AWAITING THEM ABOARD THE BLOCKADING SQUADRONS.

I have included recipes in this section that were prepared by naval forces of both navies, North and South. The reader is reminded that crews of naval forces on both sides stationed close inshore as well as on the Mississippi River Basin, took opportunities to go ashore to hunt or trade. The recipes for such dishes as possum, squirrel, and pigeon included here reflect that welcomed source of fresh meat.

Also of note is the fact that some of the recipes still do not list quantities for some of the ingredients. These have either been lost over time, or the originator of the recipe cooked using knowledge based on experience rather than precise measurements.

Last, I have included two recipes for punches made of spirits because officers were still allowed to have hard liquor during formal social events, even though the enlisted men had lost their grog rations. In time, officers would also lose this right as the conservative elements in Congress continued to press for prohibition in the military services. Once again, I have copied the recipes exactly as I found them in the myriad of sources used in my research.

Some of the recipes were tested in the kitchens of the Culinary Arts Center at San Diego High School.

HOTCHPOTCH

This recipe was tested in the kitchens at the Culinary Arts by students who found it to be rather bland and in need of additional seasonings.

Ingredients:

– 3 quarts water

– 1 cup rice or barley

– Chopped vegetables at hand (onions, carrots, turnips, parsnips, cabbage, parsley)

– Salt and pepper to taste

– 2 tablespoons butter

Instructions:

– Add grain to water and boil for a few minutes.

– Add whatever vegetables you choose to make a thick soup.

– Add seasonings and butter.

– Simmer until thickened and vegetables are well cooked, about 1 hour.

GUMBO

This recipe was tested in the kitchens at the Culinary Arts Center at San Diego High School. The students found this meal to be both tasty and to have a pleasing combination of texture and color. Their modifications to the recipe are noted below.

Ingredients:

– 1 chicken plucked and cleaned

– 1 veal shin

– 2 carrots, sliced

– 2 turnips, sliced

– 1 whole onion, peeled

– 6 quarts water

– 2 onions, sliced

– 3 tablespoons butter

– 2 tablespoons flour

– 3 quarts oysters

– 3 tablespoons gumbo filé

– Boiled rice for serving

Instructions:

– Place the first six ingredients in a large pot and bring water to a boil.

– Boil for 5 hours. *(Students recommend simmering for 2-3 hours)*

– Remove the chicken and cut into small pieces. (Keep the broth.)

– In a skillet, sauté the sliced onions in the butter until browned.

– Remove onions from pan and set aside.

– Fry the chicken in the seasoned butter until browned.

– Remove chicken and set aside.

– Return onions to the skillet, shake the flour over them and stir.

– Add the onions and the chicken to the liquid in the pot and boil for 1/2 hour.

– Wash the oysters and add them to the soup, bring to a boil and add the gumbo filé. *(Students left out the oysters.)*

– Reduce to a simmer for no more than 10 minutes. *(Students heated for only 5 minutes.)*

– Serve with a large spoonful of boiled rice.

COMMISSARY BEEF STEW

Ingredients:

- 2 lbs. beef roast cut into 2-inch square and 1-inch think cubes
- Salt and pepper
- Small amount of pork fat or lard
- Water to cover meat
- Handful of flour
- 2 onions, quartered
- 4 potatoes, peeled and quartered
- 1 tablespoon vinegar
- *(You may add other vegetables, if available)*

Instructions:

- Sprinkle meat with salt and pepper to taste.
- Place meat in a frying pan with pork fat or lard and fry until well browned, but not fully cooked.
- Empty meat into a kettle and cover with water.
- Add flour, onions, and potatoes.
- Cover and simmer slowly over moderate heat for 3 1/2 hours, skimming any fat that rises to the top.
- Stir in vinegar and serve.

RED FLANNEL HASH

Ingredients:

- 4-5 beets peeled
- 4-5 potatoes peeled
- 1 lb. beef cut into 1-inch cubes
- 3 small onions, chopped
- Small amount of pork fat
- Salt and pepper
- Small amount of water or milk

Instructions:

- Boil the beets and potatoes until soft, then drain and set aside.
- Brown the beef and onions in pork fat in a large skillet.
- Dice the beets and potatoes, and mix them into the meat mixture.
- Salt and pepper to taste.
- Pour in enough water or milk to moisten the hash slightly.
- Mash down the mixture with a spoon or spatula and fry on each side until browned.

BUBBLE AND SQUEAK

Students found this recipe easy to prepare and quite tasty. Nothing like a hearty, well-spiced bowl of corned beef and cabbage! (Note that the students added measurements for some of the ingredients.

Ingredients:

- 1/2 lb. of corned or salted beef, sliced thin
- Pepper (1 teaspoon)
- Small amount of pork fat (or shortening)
- 1 head of cabbage
- Water to cover
- Salt (1 teaspoon)
- Vinegar (2 tablespoons)

Instructions:

- Fry beef in pork fat.
- Sprinkle meat with pepper.
- Boil cabbage in just enough water to cover until soft.
- Drain cabbage, dry and chop finely and season with salt, pepper and vinegar.
- Serve a piece of beef with a good helping of cabbage.

SODA BISCUITS

Ingredients:

– ½ lb. butter
– 1 pint milk
– 1 teaspoon baking soda
– ½ lb. sugar
– 2 lbs. flour
– Flour for baking pan

Instructions:

– Melt the butter in the milk over low heat, adding the baking soda to the mixture.
– Gradually stir in the sugar and set aside.
– Sift the flour, then make a depression in the center and stir in the milk and butter mixture.
– Knead for 15 minutes, and then roll out until ½ inch thick.
– Using a tin can or cup, punch out small, round cakes, perforate with a fork, and set them on a floured cookie sheet.
– Bake in a 400-degree oven for 10 minutes or until light brown.

PORK AND BEANS

Ingredients:

– 2 lbs of salt or pickled pork, soaked overnight in water
– 2 qts. dried beans, soaked overnight in water
– Water, as noted

Instructions:

– After draining, place the pork in a pot with cold water and bring to a boil.
– Boil the pork until tender, about 3 hours, skimming off fat from surface of water.
– Drain the beans and cover with water and bring to a boil.
– Boil beans until they begin to split and are soft.
– Drain the pork and put it in the bottom of a roasting pan.
– Drain the beans, reserving some of the water.
– Cover the pork with the beans, adding some of the water from the beans.
– Cover the pan and bake in a 375-degree oven for about one hour and the top is brown.

PORK SOUP WITH VEGETABLES

Ingredients:

– 2 lbs. lean pork cut into 1-inch cubes
– 2 Tbs. pork fat for frying
– 4 quarts salted water
– 1 lb. dehydrated mixed vegetables
– Salt, pepper, and vinegar to taste
– 1 lb. stale bread, cut into 2-inch cubes

Instructions:

– Add the pork to hot fat in a skillet.
– Brown the meat, turning often.
– Place pork in the boiling, salted water.
– Boil on medium heat for 15 minutes.
– Add the dehydrated vegetables and boil for 90 minutes.
– Remove any fat from the surface and add salt, pepper and vinegar to taste.
– Add the stale bread and boil over low heat for 15 minutes and serve.

SHEEP HEAD SOUP

(As can be seen from the ingredients, this entrée was reserved for officers after the spirits ration was eliminated in 1862.)

Ingredients:

- 1 sheep's liver
- 1 sheep's lungs
- 1 gallon water
- 1 onion, sliced
- 2-3 carrots, sliced
- 1-2 turnips, chopped
- 1/2 lb. pearl barley
- Salt and pepper to taste
- 1 sheep's head, skinned
- Butter cut into small pieces and rolled in flour
- 1/2 cup sherry

Instructions:

- Dice the liver and lungs and place in a large pot.
- Add the next six ingredients and bring to a boil.
- Cook until done (?)
- Add the sheep's head and continue to boil until all the meat is tender.
- Remove the head and strain the broth.
- Allow broth to cool and skim fat from surface.
- Return the broth to the heat.
- When the broth is hot enough, drop the floured butter into the broth until thickened.
- Add the sherry and serve the thickened broth with the cold sheep's head on separate plates

FRIED RABBIT

Ingredients:

- 1/3 cup lard
- 1 rabbit, skinned, cleaned, and jointed
- 1 cup flour
- 1 teaspoon salt
- 1 teaspoon pepper
- 1 onion, chopped
- 1 cup beef stock
- 1 tablespoon cider vinegar
- 2/3 cup cream

Instructions:

- Heat the lard in a large skillet.
- Dredge rabbit in flour, salt and pepper.
- Fry rabbit pieces in hot lard until golden brown, turning once.
- Pour off excess fat and add onion, beef stock, and vinegar.
- Simmer, covered for 1 hour, or until rabbit is tender.
- Remove rabbit from the pan and keep warm.
- Pour cream into skillet and stir, scraping up bits stuck to the pan.
- Cook until think gravy has formed.
- Pour gravy over rabbit and serve.

SQUIRREL

Ingredients:

- 1 skinned and cleaned squirrel
- 1/4 cup flour
- Lard
- 1 onion, sliced
- 2 small potatoes, quartered
- 1 carrot, sliced
- Salt
- Pepper

Instructions:

- Dredge squirrel in flour and fry in hot lard until browned.
- Place in a pan and cover with water, simmering about 1 hour.
- Add vegetables and salt and pepper to taste.
- Simmer for 30 minutes and serve.

POSSUM WITH SWEET POTATOES

Ingredients:

- 1 possum, skinned, head and feet removed.
- Salt
- 8 sweet potatoes
- 2 tablespoons butter
- 1 tablespoon sugar
- 1/2 doz. strips bacon
- Thyme
- Marjoram

Instructions:

- Wash possum thoroughly in heavily salted water.
- Place possum in deep pan with a few cups of water, cover, and stew for at least 1 hour.
- Place butter, sugar, and enough water to cover sweet potatoes in a pan.
- Boil sweet potatoes until just barely soft.
- Drain the sweet potatoes and transfer them to the pot, arranging them around the possum.
- Lay bacon strips over possum and sprinkle herbs on top of all.
- Bake in 400-degree oven basting frequently until all is done.

FISH CHOWDER

Ingredients:

- 2 tablespoons oil
- 1 onion, finely diced
- 1/4 lb. salt pork, sliced thin
- 2 large fish, such as cod or catfish, cleaned and cubed
- 1/2 lb. potatoes, cubed
- Salt
- Pepper
- Water
- 4 tablespoons butter
- 1/2 cup flour
- 1 cup milk

Instructions:

- Heat oil in skillet until hot.
- Sauté onion and salt pork in oil.
- In separate pan, combine fish, potatoes, salt and pepper.
- Just cover with water and simmer for 15 minutes.
- In another pan, make a white sauce of the butter, flour, and milk.
- Add the onion and salt pork to the white sauce.
- Spoon out fish and potatoes into bowls and serve with white sauce.

POTTED PIGEON

Ingredients:

- 3 fat pigeons, plucked and cleaned
- Hardtack, crushed
- 2 eggs
- 9 tablespoons butter
- 1 1/2 teaspoon marjoram
- 3 small pieces salt pork
- 6 tablespoons flour
- Water

Instructions:

- Mix together crushed hardtack, eggs and 6 Tbs. butter.
- Spoon stuffing loosely into each bird's cavity along with a piece of salt pork.
- Dust pigeons with flour and place in roasting pan
- Add just enough water to cover the pigeons.
- Add 3 tablespoons of butter and stew over moderate heat for 90 minutes.

BOILED CHICKEN WITH OYSTERS

Ingredients:

– 1 large chicken, cleaned and plucked

– 12 oysters, shucked and washed

– 1 egg, beaten

– 1 tablespoon flour

– 1 tablespoon butter, melted

– cream

Instructions:

– Stuff the cavity of the chicken with the oysters and close.

– Place the chicken, cavity down, in a close-fitting jar or pot.

– Place jar or pot in boiling water and boil for 90 minutes.

– Remove the jar or pot from the boiling water and pour the juices into a small pan.

– Add the egg, flour, and butter and heat over low heat, adding the cream until a thick sauce is formed.

– Remove the oysters from the cavity and serve them with the chicken, covered with sauce.

KENTUCKY STEW

Students testing this recipe used only beef and pork, eliminating the mutton, lamb, squirrel, or rabbit. They found their final product to be rather bland. Maybe if they had included all of the ingredients their final product might have been a bit more tasty.

Ingredients:

– 6 tomatoes, chopped

– 6 ears fresh corn, kernels cut from the cob

– Assorted vegetables such as onions, okra, or green beans

– 1 lb. beef

– 1 lb. mutton or lamb

– 1/2 lb. pork

– 1 whole chicken, cut into 1 1/2 inch pieces

– 1-2 squirrels, if available, or a rabbit

– Salt and pepper

Instructions:

– In a large pot, place the tomatoes, corn, and other vegetables of choice.

– Add all meats to pot.

– Cover with water and bring to a boil.

– Continue boiling, adding water as necessary, until the meat is falling apart and ingredients are blended into a thick soup.

– Salt and pepper heavily.

– Serve, ideally, in a tin cup.

U.S.S. HARTFORD DANDYFUNK

Ingredients:

- ½ doz. hardtack biscuits
- Cold water
- ½ lb. salt pork, cut into small bits
- ½ cup molasses

Instructions:

- Soak hardtack biscuits in cold water until softened.
- Mix in salt pork and molasses.
- Bake in oven at 350 degrees until well browned.

FRIED PIG'S FEET

Ingredients:

- Flour as needed
- Water
- ½ teaspoon salt
- 1 egg
- Pig's feet, washed and dried
- Lard

Instructions:

- Combine flour, water, salt, and egg to make a thick batter.
- Dip washed and dried pig's feet into batter until well covered.
- Fry in hot lard until well browned.
- May be served with butter and vinegar.

BREAD PUDDING

Students were unanimous in their approval of both the taste and texture of this simple recipe. Again, students added more precise measurements where needed.

Ingredients:

- Several slices of stale bread (10)
- Milk to cover (about 1 cup)
- 3 eggs
- dash salt
- 1 tablespoons molasses

Instructions:

- Crumble the bread into a bowl.
- Cover bread with milk, and soak overnight (or until milk is completely absorbed by the bread).
- Beat eggs until frothy, and fold into bread and milk mixture.
- Add seasonings to taste.
- Tie mixture in a waterproof bag and place in a pot of boiling water. *Students placed the mixture into a glass casserole, and covered it with foil. They then placed the casserole into a larger vessel and poured water into the larger vessel until it was half-way up the side of the casserole.*
- Boil for one hour. *Students baked their pudding for one hour until set.*

BREAKFAST SCOUSE

Ingredients:
- 4 potatoes, peeled and quartered
- 1/2 dozen hardtack, crumbled
- Butter for frying

Instructions:
- Boil potatoes until cooked through.
- Pour off water and add hardtack.
- Fry in a skillet until brown and crisp.

GINGER BEER

Ingredients:
- 1 pint molasses
- 2 teaspoons ground ginger
- 2 qts. boiling water
- 2 qts. cold water
- 1 pt. liquid yeast

Instructions:
- In a 4-quart pot combine the molasses and ginger.
- Add the boiling water and stir until ingredients are well mixed.
- Add cold water and stir until mixture is lukewarm.
- Cover and store in warm place overnight.
- Bottle.

SPREAD EAGLE PUNCH

Ingredients:
- 1 bottle Scotch whiskey
- 1 bottle rye whiskey
- Grated peel of two lemons
- 1 pound granulated sugar
- 1 pt. boiling water

Instructions:
- Combine whiskeys in large bowl.
- Add other ingredients and stir until the sugar is dissolved.
- Drink.

BRANDY SHRUB

Ingredients:
- 2 qts. brandy
- Juice of 5 lemons
- Zest of 2 lemons
- 1 qt. sherry
- 2 lbs. sugar

Instructions:
- Pour the brandy into a 5-quart bowl and lemon juice.
- Add lemon zest and stir.
- Cover and let sit for 3 days.
- Add sherry and sugar, and stir until sugar is dissolved.
- Strain and serve.

Chapter 3

NAVAL MESSING ENTERS THE MODERN AGE

The Spanish-American War

THE WEATHER WAS WARM AND CLEAR as the ships of the United States Navy prepared once again for war on April 24th, 1898. The waters of Victoria Harbor, between Hong Kong and Kowloon, the New Territories of China, were crisscrossed by the wakes of small boats as Chinese merchants raced their craft about the harbor selling last minute provisions to the ships of the Asiatic Squadron. Frank May, Ship's Cook First Class aboard the *U.S.S. Olympia,* smiled as he thought about how the Chinese always knew when the fleet was sailing. It was another of the mysteries of the Far East; how those ashore knew when the fleet was arriving or departing, even though the squadron's orders remained sealed in the Commanding Officer's Cabin.

But a person would have to be both blind and deaf to miss the fact that the four protected cruisers, two gunboats, and single revenue cutter floating on the relatively calm waters of the bay were there for nothing other than a showing of the flag. Captain Gridley had informed the crew of the *U.S.S. Olympia* that the U.S. Congress had adopted a Joint Resolution for a Declaration of War against Spain on April 19th. After it was signed by President McKinley on April 20th, a state of war was said to exist between the United States and Spain. The order had been passed to refuel and replenish the ships in order that they might get under way at a moment's notice for Mirs Bay, just south of their present position. Only a fool would fail to realize that Mirs Bay lay only a few days sailing from the Philippines. And even the newest Landsman aboard the fleet's flagship knew that the Spanish fleet was last reported at anchor in Manila Bay.

Petty Officer May's thoughts were interrupted by the sound of Ah Song, the Wardroom Cook, hailing the owner of one of several small boats filled with fresh fruit and vegetables. Waiving wildly, he motioned for his countryman to draw up alongside so Song could inspect the goods being offered for sale. Petty Officer May noticed with interest that Ta Zee Ding, Commodore Dewey's personal chef, was also leaning over the ship's rail and shouting at the merchant. The *Olympia* had five Chinese and one Japanese cook aboard to prepare meals for the ship's officers. With only 31 officers and warrant officers aboard, that made one cook for every 5 officers. May smiled as he thought of how nice it would be to have that many cooks in his galley, where he and Ship's Cook 4th Class Joe Tomlinson struggled to cook three meals a day for the ship's 387 enlisted men.

After the small boat pulled alongside, Song and his Assistant Cook quickly scrambled down the side of the ship and began rummaging through the produce in the violently rocking craft. There followed some haggling and waving of arms by both sides until a deal was finally struck. Money exchanged hands, and the two cooks just as quickly clambered back aboard. By the looks of the produce neatly arranged in baskets tucked tightly in the bumboat, it was obvious that the officers would continue to eat well aboard the squadron's flagship. In a few minutes more, Wardroom and Warrant Officer's Mess Stewards began to load the fresh vegetables aboard and stow them below in one of the ship's refrigerated storerooms.

May thought wryly, "The officers may have fresh vegetables at the wardroom table tonight, but there won't be any for the rest of the crew of the *Olympia*." The ship's officers obtained their rations by signing long-term catering contracts with international firms, many of them British, that supplied the ships when they were in foreign ports. The officer who managed the wardroom mess made up menus for the three hot meals offered to the ship's officers each day. The menus were then presented to the Asian

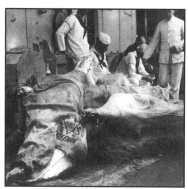

cooks who worked in the various officers' galleys. They, in turn, listed the ingredients they needed to prepare the individual dishes. Once the mess manager received these lists, additional funds could be made available to the appropriate cooks to purchase items needed from local merchants either ashore or afloat. The officers no longer had to keep live animals aboard as a source of fresh meat and eggs as they had done during the Revolutionary War. Refrigeration had solved the problem of storing special cuts of meat and poultry.

Petty Officer May was the head cook for the 18 separate enlisted messes aboard the *Olympia*. Each mess, made up of 20 men, was served by a single mess cook who lined up with others to draw unprepared rations measured out by an officer assigned by the ship's captain. Each mess cook then prepared some memorized recipe using the issued rations, plus any additional ingredients stored in the mess' ration box. When ready to have their ration cooked, the mess cooks lined up once again at the galley to pass their preparations to the cooks who then arranged the food in the ship's ovens and pots as best they could. One-fourth of the ration was still commuted in cash to the mess cooks, who were allowed to use this money to augment the standard issue rations drawn from the ship's stores. These men vied with the cooks from the wardroom to make purchases from the merchants attempting to sell fresh food to the ships in the fleet. Purchased items such as fresh bread, cakes, and pies were stored in each mess' ration box while fresh eggs and fruit were placed in well-marked bags and stored in the limited space available in the refrigerated store rooms. Thus, as in the older navy, each mess was still dependent upon the skill and attention of the man assigned to serve the mess, even though the actual cooking of the food was still the responsibility of the ship's cooks.

In addition to the officers' wardroom and the 18 enlisted men's messes, the *Olympia's* 17 chief petty officers had their own mess cook who also drew their rations from the ship's galley. The chiefs not only paid their mess cook an extra fee to be especially attentive to the preparation of their meals, they also assessed themselves an additional fee each month to augment their commuted rations. Dining almost as well as the ship's officers, they took their meals separately from the rest of the enlisted crew in a small mess located near their quarters aft.

FRESH BAKED BREAD AND SHINING UTENSILS ARE DISPLAYED BY MESS MEN ABOARD THE *U.S.S. OLYMPIA.*

Food storage and preparation had changed in the U.S. Navy since the Civil War. In the intervening 33 years, refrigeration had moved beyond the rudimentary ice chest lashed to the deck of a monitor. Refrigeration units installed aboard could keep entire store rooms filled with sides of beef and pork at a constant 32 degrees Fahrenheit. Along with the disappearance of the ice chests, the cask of "salt horse" was now gone from its place lashed to the foot of the mainmast. Individual messes no longer ate their food from a canvas tarp spread on the deck, but instead sat on benches around wooden tables that were lashed to the overhead when not in use. The metal plates and cups of agate wear, issued as part of a sailor's initial outfit, would soon be replaced by heavy white glass dishes and cups. Each member of the mess now ate his meal using a personal set of eating utensils, consisting of a knife, fork and spoon, also of standard navy issue.

At the dawn of the 20th century, the preparation of food for the enlisted ranks in the U.S. Navy was to change dramatically. Under the guidance of such far-sighted officers as Lt. Benton C. Decker, aboard the *U.S.S. Indiana*, and Paymaster George P. Dyer aboard the *U.S.S. Missouri*, the numerous individual messes left to the best (or worst) intentions of individual mess cooks were to became a thing of the past. The 18 individual messes aboard the *U.S.S. Olympia* would disappear, to be replaced by one general mess responsible for the feeding of all 387 enlisted men aboard. Mess cooks would no longer have a hand in the drawing of the unprepared rations, and their role in the actual preparation of the meals was greatly reduced. New methods of food preparation were adopted and recipes were standardized and published throughout the fleets in order that the quality of meals might be universally improved.

Upon adopting the general mess system, the pay officer of a ship was designated the Commissary, or provisioning officer. This officer was "solely responsible for the purchase and preparation of the food for the general mess, the care of the stores, and the judicious expenditure of mess funds." Assisted by a Commissary Steward who kept an account of all of the stores of the general mess, this officer was answerable to the ship's captain in all matters concerning the purchasing, storage, issuing, and cooking of the crew's rations. The wardroom continued to be managed by a separate officer known as the Wardroom Treasurer.

THE ANSWER TO THE RIDDLE "WHO SLEEPS BELOW WHERE HE EATS AND EATS BELOW WHERE HE SLEEPS?" CAN BE ANSWERED BY A CLOSE INSPECTION OF THESE PICTURES.

The ship's Chief Commissary Steward was a Chief Petty Officer who was in charge of the operation of the general mess. He made out the daily bill of fare and presented it to the Commissary in order to draw the necessary stores for issue directly to the ship's cooks. He was responsible for directing the preparation of the food as well as its issue to the mess men, who were now relegated to the job of transporting the prepared food from the galley to the individual messes located throughout the ship. The Chief Commissary Steward was also expected to assist the Commissary in the purchase, receipt, storage and inspection of all foodstuffs belonging to the enlisted general mess.

Although the Chief Commissary Steward was responsible for the preparation of the daily menu, he left the day-to-day operation of the galley to the Senior Cook. This lower-ranked petty officer had the responsibility of superintending the cooking of all meals, inspecting the food and the equipment used in its preparation, and the performance of the cooks and bakers working under him. He was responsible for assigning these relatively junior enlisted ratings to specific duties such as "meat cook," "vegetable cook," and "baker." One man, in addition to his other duties, was held responsible for the preparation of the coffee and tea

By the turn of the century the quality of navy food had improved somewhat, but sailors were still eating some of the same basic rations their predecessors had been served during the Civil War. The enlisted crew might have vegetables in their stews and fruit in their puddings, but neither would be fresh and crisp like those at the wardroom table. Fresh ingredients would be canned and overcooked until every last vitamin had been squeezed out of them, or dried and pressed until the last drop of moisture was

CONDITIONS ON THE ENLISTED BERTHING DECK WERE VERY CONFINING, WITH SAILORS FORCED TO FIND SPACE WHERE THEY COULD BEYOND THE 24 INCHES ALLOCATED FOR EACH MAN'S HAMMOCK.

gone. And though there may have been some fresh beef and pork in the ration, most of the meat the crew would consume had been pressed and then boiled in large tins. When opened by the cook, this tinned beef or pork barely resembled the meat of the animal from which it came. Ship's biscuit was still listed as a part of the standard ship's ration, but by the turn of the century it would disappear with the exception of being a part of the emergency rations in a ship's boats. In its place, flour that could be baked into fresh bread, rolls, cakes, and the crusts for pies was introduced to the ration.

SUCH INNOVATIONS AS THE HOBART MIXER AND THE AUTOMATIC POTATO PEELER MADE THE COOKS' JOB MUCH EASIER IN THE NEW NAVY.

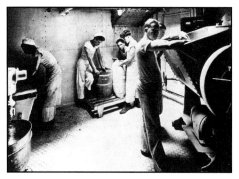

The Campbell Food Company was still supplying the navy with large tins of pre-cooked pork and beans, while other companies were experimenting with improved methods of preserving vegetables and canning prepared gravies and sauces for sale to the government. The addition of freshly baked bread, fresh potatoes, carrots, citrus fruits and tinned fruit juices helped to nourish a healthier and happier crew that could better withstand the arduous days at sea as well as the monotony of long periods in port with only a minimum of shore liberty. The involvement of the Naval Medical Services Corps on the Naval Provisioning Board allowed doctors to give input concerning nutrition and the reduction of the fat content in the standard ration. This involvement also contributed greatly to the prevention and containment of disease aboard ships at sea by implementing improvements in sanitation in food preparation areas.

But refrigeration, canned food, and a reduction of fat in the sailor's diet weren't the only improvements in the navy mess. Under the new system, waste was drastically reduced by the economy of scale. No longer was food preparation assigned to 40-odd poorly trained individuals, chosen mostly on the basis that they were not proficient at the duties assigned to the members of their mess. Instead,

MESS MEN ABOARD AN ARMORED CRUISER POSING WITH SOME OF THE TOOLS OF THEIR TRADE.

a single ration was being issued to all, based upon a menu presented to a trained cook and approved by the officer in charge of the mess. Ships could now make purchases in quantity, while previously mess men were left on their own to determine how the commuted portion of the mess ration was to be spent. No longer would mess men squander their fellow crewmen's mess funds to finance their personal adventures ashore or use the funds to cover bets in ship-wide competitions. No longer would the crew experience the monotony of the same food served day after day according to whether it was "Beef Wednesday" or "Pork Thursday." Now the ship's crew would be served a wholesome diet of nutritious food prepared by trained galley crews.

Other changes in the enlisted mess during the early part of the twentieth century include the 1902 publication of the first Navy Cookbook, produced by the Navy Paymaster General and published by the Bureau of Supplies and Accounts. This cookbook contained seven recipes for soups and chowders, four for fish, twenty-three for meats, three each for fowl, eggs, and stew, thirteen for vegetables, nine for desserts, three for meat or fruit pies, and one for the baking of bread. It is notable that among the new recipes, "plum duff," an old navy stand-by since the Revolutionary War was still a favorite of the enlisted mess. (Also of note is that the first issue of the *Blue Jacket's Manual*, the book introducing basic naval concepts and skills needed by recruits, was published that same year.) An Act of Congress signed on July 1, 1902, increased the daily ration of both vegetables and meat, adding tomatoes to the ration.

WITH THE INTRODUCTION OF THE DISH WASHING MACHINE, EATING UTENSILS NO LONGER WERE COVERED BY A SHEEN OF GREASE.

In 1904, the first dishwashing machine was installed aboard the *U.S.S. Missouri*. Gone at last was the previously tolerated film of grease on cutlery and dishes. Rules were published concerning the control of flies in storage and cooking areas as well as the covering of perishables such as butter, syrup, vinegar and catsup. Mechanization spread throughout the fleet, and soon potato peelers and mashers, meat grinders and slicers, dough mixers, and even ice cream freezers began to appear in ships' galleys. In 1906, Congress added eggs, jam, and spices to the ration while authorizing "an over-issue of any article in the Navy ration so long as there is an equal under-issue of the same value of some other articles." By the time it had moved into the second decade of the 20th Century and was faced with its first war fought on a global basis, the U.S. Navy was well on its way to having the best-fed fighting force in the world.

THE FOLLOWING BILL OF FARE IS TYPICAL OF THE MEALS SERVED IN THE
NAVY AT THE TURN OF THE CENTURY:

REVEILLE: *Hot coffee*

BREAKFAST: *Boiled eggs, liver and bacon, coffee, bread and butter.*

DINNER: *Fresh corned beef and cabbage, potatoes, new onions and
radishes, coffee, bread and butter.*

SUPPER: *Chicken Stew, tea, bread and butter.*

– *Condensed milk and sugar were provided for the tea and coffee.*
– *Vinegar and catsup were stocked in every mess box.*

Sunday dinner may have included roast pork, jelly, fresh green peas, new potatoes,
and pie.

(The reader should note the introduction of two additional hot meals each day
instead of the single hot meal augmented by ship's biscuit and leftovers eaten by sailors
in the earlier navy.)

An entry from the log of the *U.S.S. Brooklyn* (with a complement of 480 officers
and men) gives a sense of the variety of food items available to the crew by listing the
provisions loaded aboard for a period of one month during the Spanish-American War:

PROVISIONS

Bread	6,000 pounds	Bacon	480 pounds	Macaroni	300 pounds
Yeast	35 pounds	Catsup	480 quarts	Beans	300 gallons
Sugar	3,000 pounds	Fruit, dried	100 pounds	Potatoes	400 bushels
Coffee	900 pounds	Pepper	30 pounds	Onions	12 bushels
Condensed Milk	300 pints	Pickles	300 pounds	Turnips	20 bushels
Tea	100 pounds	Syrup	30 gallons	Cabbage	600 heads
Butter	1,000 pounds	Pork chops	900 pounds	Clams	120 quarts
Lard	200 pounds	Sausages	300 pounds	Flavors	12 pints
Beef, fresh	8,000 pounds	Mackerel, salted	400 pounds	Salt	300 pounds
Fish, fresh	2,000 pounds	Pig's feet	500 pounds	Curry powder	24 pounds
Pork, salt	1,800 pounds	Meats, tinned	800 pounds	Vinegar	30 gallons
Beef, salt	1,200 pounds	Bologna	240 pounds	Eggs	1,500
Liver	800 pounds	Cheese	240 pounds		
Ham	900 pounds	Rice	800 pounds		

Life at sea was harsh, and crews were confined to their ships for long periods. After arriving at a foreign port, liberty ashore was limited because captains feared for the safety of their crews in what sometimes proved to be a hostile environment ashore. Pay was poor for the average sailor, and what he might have in his pocket seldom carried him beyond the waterfront dives where he could be injured in a fight or even killed. There was also the question of whether or not some crew members might willingly return to the confines of the foc'sle after experiencing life ashore in an exotic foreign port. Although the grog ration had been discontinued during the American Civil War, many naval captains allowed contracted vendors to come aboard with beer to be portioned out to the crew under the watchful eye of an officer. This helped to keep the "men forward," somewhat mollified, during long, hot days in port.

The recipes I have chosen from the "General Mess Manual and Cook Book for Use on Board Vessels of the United States Navy" are representative of the general categories mentioned in my previous reference to this document. Each recipe is designed to feed 100 men, and the contents thereof are based upon a ration set by law of 30 cents per man per day. I have copied the recipes exactly as they appear in the cookbook, which includes cooking instructions within the list of ingredients. The reader may note that exact measurements of spices are apparently left to the best judgment of the cook, and cooking times are sometimes left out completely. I have also been careful to copy the language and punctuation exactly as printed in the original text. (All "Notes" are copied verbatim from the cookbook.)

SAILORS DRINK THEIR BEER RATIONS ON THE COVERED DECK OF THEIR ARMED CRUISER WHILE THE COMMISSARY OFFICER AND A CIVILIAN CONTRACTOR KEEP A WATCHFUL EYE TO MAKE SURE ALL THE EMPTY BOTTLES ARE RETURNED TO THE CASES.

FISH CHOWDER

Instructions:

Cut up 10 pounds of salt pork in 1-inch cakes and render out in frying pan until brown. Cut 50 pounds of potatoes and 20 pounds of onions in small pieces and place them with the pork in 12 ½ gallons of water. Boil 30 pounds of fresh cod or halibut until tender, let it cool, remove all bones and add to the above. Season with salt and pepper, add 1 gallon of milk, if obtainable, and boil for ten minutes.

Note. The potatoes for chowders may be prepared the night before and kept in fresh water.

BAKED FISH

Instructions:

Soak 10 pounds of stale bread in cold water, and when soft press all the water out. Season with pepper, salt, and thyme and spread a thin layer on the bottom of well-greased baking pans. Clean and wipe dry 75 pounds of fish, place in the pans and dredge with flour, pepper, and salt, adding a small quantity of tomatoes or tomato juice. Place in a moderately hot oven for about forty-five minutes, or until done.

FISH CAKES

Instructions:

Soak 25 pounds of codfish over night in fresh water. Boil for an hour and a quarter, drain off water, remove bones, and chop up. Boil 50 pounds of potatoes, and to them add the fish, together with one pound of butter, 6 eggs, and 1 ounce of pepper. Mash all together thoroughly, make into cakes, and place in pans in the oven to brown.

Note Fish cakes may be fried in the manner prescribed for frying fish. That process is provided, as follows.

FRYING FISH:

Instructions:

Place a pan of drippings, butter, or lard on the fire and let it come to the boiling point. Fry the fish in this from eight to ten minutes, turning after the first three minutes.

BEEF SOUP

Instructions:

Use 90 pounds of soup meat (as much bone as possible); let simmer for two hours, then remove meat and add vegetables as follows: One quart of barley, 6 pounds of carrots, 3 pounds of onions, 2 pounds of turnips (the vegetables having been cleaned and cut into strips), and allow the soup to boil for one hour. Season with pepper, salt, cloves, and spices; mix flour and water to the consistency of a syrup and stir in, while boiling, a sufficient quantity to thicken it. After boiling for ten minutes longer the soup is ready to serve. After the beef is removed it should be kept hot until served.

BEEF STEW

Instructions:

Wash 60 pounds of beef in water to which a little vinegar and salt has been added, and then cut into small pieces. Place in the copper (steam kettle) with 10 gallons of water and boil for one hour. Slice up 40 pounds of potatoes, 10 pounds of carrots, and 15 pounds of onions (the potatoes and onions being cut into quarters) and add to the above. Allow the whole to boil until the vegetables are done and then add 10 pounds of tomatoes. Season with pepper and salt and allow it to simmer for twenty minutes.

BEEF STEW

(As prepared by culinary arts students at San Diego High School)

Ingredients:

- 2 tomatoes
- 1 lb. beef
- 4 carrots
- 1 yellow onion
- 2 stalks celery
- 2 potatoes
- 1/4 c. flour
- Salt and pepper to taste

Instructions:

- Rinse and core tomatoes, cut into small cubes, set aside.
- Trim fat from beef, cut into small cubes, peel and cut carrots into rounds, chop onion and celery, and peel and dice potatoes.
- Place beef and vegetables in a 4 qt. saucepan with 8 c. water.
- Bring water to a boil, reduce heat and allow meat and vegetables to simmer until vegetables are tender and meat is cooked, about 20-25 minutes.
- To thicken stew, place flour in a mixing bowl, pour 1 c. of the broth over the flour and whisk until smooth. Add to the stew, stirring constantly.
- Stir in tomatoes.
- When stew thickens, serve.

POT ROAST

Instructions:

Place 75 pounds of lean beef in pots with 2 pounds of beef dripping. Cut up 1 quart of onions, 6 carrots, and 6 bay leaves, and add them to the beef. Place the pots on the galley (stove), and allow them to simmer for twenty minutes. Turn the meat frequently, taking care that it does not stick to the bottom of the pots. Throw in 1 quart of dry flour, and season well with pepper and salt, stirring thoroughly; then add 2 quarts of boiling water, continually stirring, and allow it to simmer for twenty minutes longer. Then cover the whole with boiling water, let cook until tender, and serve.

FRESH ROAST BEEF

Ingredients:

Take 90 pounds of ribs, wipe with a towel soaked in salt water, dry thoroughly and place in pans, adding 3 onions and 3 carrots sliced up. Dredge the meat with pepper, salt, and flour, using the flour liberally. Place pans in the oven, and after thirty minutes baste with 2 quarts of boiling water. Bake for an hour and a half, watching meat carefully and keeping plenty of water in the pans with which to baste. When cooked, remove from the oven, stir a little more flour into the essence of the meat, add 2 more quarts of boiling water, let it simmer for five minutes in the oven or on top of the galley, carve meat and serve with the gravy.

Note: Top sirloin or cross ribs can also be roasted.

ROAST TURKEY, CHICKEN, GEESE AND DUCKS

Ingredients:

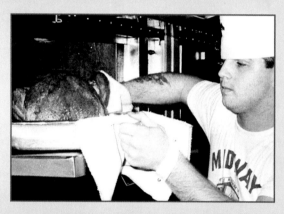

Ninety pounds of fowl will be required. In dressing be careful not to break the gall. Wash thoroughly inside and out in salt water and dry. Season well inside with salt and pepper and fill the cavity with the stuffing prescribed for roast veal in the case of turkey and chicken, and for goose and ducks the one given below. Place in dry pans, dredging well with flour, and roast for twenty minutes. Then baste frequently with hot water, turning them twice, and allow them to roast two and a half hours.

Gravy is made as follows: Take the hearts, livers, and gizzards, wash them off thoroughly and place them in 2 quarts of cold water. Chop 1 pound of onions and place the whole together on a fire in a saucepan; cook for one hour, take out hearts, livers, and gizzards, saving the juice. Chop up the giblets fine, placing them back in the juice, and add the gravy from the pans to it. Season with salt and pepper.

STUFFING FOR ROAST VEAL, TURKEY AND CHICKEN

Ingredients:

Soak 15 pounds of stale bread in cold water and drain thoroughly; add 3 pounds of sliced onions, fried until brown, and pepper, salt, and thyme; mix all thoroughly. (Brown in oven if serving with veal, or use to stuff birds if using with turkey or chicken.)

STUFFING FOR GEESE AND DUCKS

Ingredients:

Cook 7 pounds of fried apples thirty minutes in enough water to cover them. Put 18 pounds of stale bread to soak, squeeze the water out of the bread, add the apples to it, mix together thoroughly and season with pepper and salt.

TINNED ROAST BEEF WITH MACARONI

Ingredients:

Place 2 pounds of onions, chopped fine, in a pot with $1/4$ pound of dripping and brown them on the galley. Stir in 1 pound of flour and then 2 quarts of boiling water. Add 6 pounds of tomatoes and 60 pounds of tinned beef. Add to this 6 pounds of macaroni which has been dropped into boiling water, well salted, and cooked until tender. Season with pepper and salt and simmer for twenty minutes. *Note: To prepare this dish in the coppers, proceed as follows: After the flour, onions, tomatoes and boiling water have simmered for ten minutes in a pot add them to the meat and the macaroni in the copper. Season and simmer for twenty minutes.*

BAKED PORK AND BEANS

Ingredients:

Wash thoroughly 5 $1/2$ gallons of beans and soak in cold water over night. In another pot soak 15 pounds of salt pork over night. Place the pork and beans together in pots on the fire (scoring the pork). Add water, and boil with pot covered for one hour. Season with salt and pepper. When the beans are soft add 2 pints of molasses, turn out into pans, and bake in a quick oven until brown.

HAM OMELET

Ingredients:

Fifteen pounds of ham and 22 dozen of eggs will be required. Chop ham fine. Put eggs, one at a time, in a large pan. Season with pepper. Beat eggs at least twenty minutes. Take large narrow baking pans and cover bottom with lard. When lard is hot, pour about 2 dozen well-beaten eggs into each pan. Remove from the bottom of the pan occasionally. When eggs are set, put a quantity of chopped ham along the center and fold the sides over the center.

TINNED CORN FRITTERS

Ingredients:

Sift into a dish 10 pounds of flour, 5 ounces of baking powder, and $1/2$ pound of sugar; mix with cold water to a smooth batter and add 15 pounds of tinned corn, mixing all together. Place dripping in pans on the fire and when it is smoking hot, drop in the batter by large spoonfuls and fry, turning as soon as one side is brown. After frying, bake in oven for ten minutes.

Note: The addition of a dozen eggs, when obtainable, will improve these fritters.

SAN DIEGO HIGH VERSION OF CORN FRITTERS

Ingredients:

– 6 whole ears of corn
– 1 c. flour
– 1 tsp. baking powder
– 3 Tbs. sugar
– 1 egg
– $1/2$ c. cold water

Instructions:

– Remove husk and cut corn from cob into mixing bowl.
– Sift flour, baking powder and sugar into a medium mixing bowl.
– Whisk eggs and water together, stir in flour and corn.
– Preheat a cast iron skillet with 1 inch of soybean oil.
– Fry spoonfuls of the corn batter until light brown, turn and complete cooking.
– Drain on a paper towel-lined bake pan. Keep fritters warm in 160-degree oven.

BAKED MACARONI

Instructions:

Place into a copper containing 10 gallons of boiling water 3/4 of a pound of salt. Break 50 pounds of macaroni into the copper and allow it to boil for thirty minutes. Strain off and place in well-greased pans; grate 10 pounds of cheese on top of the macaroni and bake in a hot oven for twenty minutes.

(Note. - 6 pounds of tomatoes may be added before baking if desired.)

POTATO SALAD

Instructions:

Peel and slice 30 pounds of boiled potatoes, to which add 6 pounds of onions and 2 bunches of parsley, chopped up fine, mix all together with pepper and salt. Stir in 2 quarts vinegar and 1 pint of oil and allow the salad to stand for an hour before serving.

CABBAGE

Instructions:

Cut two barrels of cabbage into quarters, wash thoroughly and put into cold water in the copper and boil for one hour. Season well with pepper and salt.

PLUM DUFF

Instructions:

Soak 25 pounds of stale bread in cold water and drain dry. Add 25 pounds of sifted flour, 5 pounds of suet chopped fine, 3 pounds of raisins, 5 pounds of sugar, 4 pounds of currants, 2 pounds of prunes, 3 tablespoonfuls of salt, 1 teaspoonful of ground cloves, 1 teaspoonful of ground cinnamon, and one wineglassful of vinegar, and mix all thoroughly with cold water. Turn the bags inside out, drop them into boiling water, render out slightly, and drop into dry flour, dredging them thoroughly. Turn the bags flour side in and fill them with the pudding, securing the opening firmly, drop into the copper in which water is boiling and cook for at least two hours. If there is sufficient time, the pudding will be improved by boiling it for three or four hours.

Note: Refer back to the recipes for Duff in Chapters One and Two to see how this recipe has changed over the years.

RICE PUDDING

Instructions:

Wash 30 pounds of rice and place in pots of cold water on the galley, letting it boil for thirty minutes. In six cans of condensed milk or 10 quarts of fresh milk dissolve 6 pounds of sugar and 2 tablespoonfuls of salt. When the rice is soft, add the milk and 5 pounds of currents, 6 pounds of raisins, and 4-dozen eggs, and mix all together. Place the pudding in greased pans, grate nutmeg over them, and bake in oven until brown.

Note: When condensed milk is used, it should be diluted to the consistency of rich fresh milk.

BREAD

Instructions:

Sift 50 pounds of flour into a large kneading pan and add about 2 pounds of hot drippings. Break ten cakes of yeast into small pieces and put into lukewarm water and stir until dissolved. Add this to the flour and drippings and also add 2 1/2 gallons of fresh water and 2 1/2 gallons of salt water lukewarm, mixing all thoroughly. Dust the dough with a thin coating of flour to prevent its crusting. Cover the pan with a cloth and stand in a warm place from four to six hours, then knead out well and make into loaves. Put in well-greased pans and bake in moderate oven for forty-five minutes.

BAKED APPLE DUMPLINGS

Instructions:

Mix 8 pounds of drippings and 15 pounds of sifted flour, rubbing it in thoroughly with the hands, add 3 tablespoonfuls of salt, mix with cold water into a stiff paste, roll out to the thickness of 1/8 of an inch and cut into 5 inch squares. Pare and core 100 apples and place one on each square of the dough. Fill the center of the apples with sugar, roll them up in the dough and bake them in a greased pan in a hot oven for thirty minutes, or until the apples become soft.

Note: The crust described above is suitable for any meat or fried pie.

Chapter 4

BEANS, BUTTER AND BULLETS
Provisioning the U.S. Navy during World War II

LIEUTENANT (JUNIOR GRADE) LANIER ANDERSON, Communications Officer of the *U.S.S. Key*, (DE-348) descended the bridge ladder slowly. It was November 14, 1944, and he had just finished the 0400 to 0800 watch as Officer of the Deck. After a quick breakfast in the wardroom, he had to complete making the latest changes in the Secret Communications Procedural Manuals the ship had received during a brief re-supply stop at Eniwetok, a small atoll in the Marshall Islands. If he was lucky, Anderson would finish this task just in time to take over the deck again for the first dog watch from 1600 to 1800.

Because he was an hour late for normal breakfast service in the wardroom, Lieutenant junior grade Anderson knew he could look forward to a meal of lukewarm leftovers put aside for him by the wardroom cook who prepared the officers' meals. After pouring some almost-scalding hot coffee from the always-full urn in the corner of the wardroom into a porcelain cup and placing it on a matching saucer on the wardroom table, he crossed to the serving window separating the galley from the wardroom and called to the steward.

"Good morning, Victor. Did you remember to hold something for me this morning?" The young officer knew the steward would have something put aside for him and his fellow officers who were standing watches during the regular meal hours of 0700, 1200 and 1700. The real question was whether or not there might be some change to the dull routine of navy fare they had all become used to during the past months of almost continuous combat in the Pacific.

"Here you are, sir," replied the steward, passing a covered plate through the window. "No surprises this morning, Lieutenant. There's ketchup in the side board and some left-over toast in the bread box."

"Thanks" replied the young officer, his voice reflecting his disappointment at seeing yet another meal consisting mostly of dehydrated food. Picking up his plate, he crossed

to the sideboard atop which he placed the porcelain plate containing a small pile of watery dehydrated scrambled eggs, some dried out fried reconstituted cubed potatoes, and resting by itself, a single, thick slice of leathery-looking SPAM, its surface dull with coagulated grease. Reaching into the sideboard, Ltjg. Anderson grasped a bottle of ketchup, opened it, and then covered the whole mess on his plate with the thick, red sauce. Opening the breadbox, he found two damp slices of toast. After placing these on his plate, he returned the ketchup to its proper place and looked for a jar of jam. After some rummaging about in the dark recesses of the sideboard, he discovered a can stamped "Jam, Mixed Berry - Concentrated." Scooping two spoonfuls of this glutinous mass onto each slice of his bread, he replaced the can, closed the sideboard, and carried the now colorful plate to the wardroom table where his now drinkable cup of coffee awaited him.

The meal eaten by Ltjg. Anderson on board the *U.S.S. Key* that morning in late 1944 was typical of the food served aboard many naval vessels during the war in the Pacific. Although destroyers and destroyer escorts were the workhorses of the fleet, the food served aboard them was notorious for its monotony. And although generally nutritious, its preparation varied from ship to ship, as in the earlier years of the navy. But there were two other factors affecting the food served aboard the *U.S.S. Key* that had not come into play prior to this period in the history of the feeding of our sailors at sea. They were the logistics involved in supplying our fleets in a two-ocean war, and the varying quality of the food supplied to particular operational units within each fleet.

Prior to World War II, United States naval operations were generally confined to a single area or ocean. Although the fleets were called upon to carry out operations in such places as the Mediterranean Sea or the South Atlantic, our navy was basically a one-ocean fleet. Arrangements with foreign countries to purchase supplies for our fleets were common, and supply ships sent to replenish the fleet could do so with relative efficiency, needing to travel moderate distances between friendly ports and the battle fleet. Commodore Dewey was able to obtain supplies in China while fighting the Spanish-American War in the Philippines.

However, in World War II, the delivery of food to our fleets which were spread across both the Atlantic and Pacific Oceans was a major challenge in maintaining the battle efficiency of our deployed naval forces. In many cases, the nearest source of supplies was more than a thousand sea-miles away from our front line units. In the Pacific, in particular, not only did the Navy have to supply its fleet units, but it had to supply massive Army and Marine Corps units deployed over the region as well. This strained the abilities of the procurement establishment ashore as well as the fleet given the responsibility for delivering these necessities of war over vast areas.

The decisions concerning how many "Bullets or Beans" to supply to the fleets was of major concern in this great struggle. It was one thing to have enough fuel and

ammunition to effectively fight the enemy, but the men manning the ships and guns had to have high quality food to sustain themselves during long periods at sea. This required that the U.S. Navy build a large fleet of supply, refrigeration, and replenishment ships to service the units both in front of and behind the battle lines in the two-ocean war.

In the early days of the war there were only four major supply points on the west coast of the United States: San Diego, San Pedro, and San Francisco in California, and Bremerton, in Washington. Our base in Hawaii stood alone in the Pacific between the continental United States and the next free ports located in Australia and New Zealand. Ships fighting in remote parts of the Pacific had to make long voyages between battle areas and safe harbors where they could replenish their supplies of ammunition and food. Some of the ships that fought in the Battle of Midway, for instance, had to sail all the way back to San Pedro, California to replenish their supplies of fuel and ammunition.

Although underway replenishment had been practiced by naval forces prior to the outbreak of hostilities, ships were only required to conduct one at-sea replenishment exercise each year to meet fleet standards. While crews were capable of completing this complex evolution, it was not generally thought to be an effective method of re-supplying the fleet units because of the limited number of supply ships available coupled with the danger encountered during the high-lining of fuel and provisions while under way in heavy seas. Only after new crews aboard a fleet of newly constructed supply ships were trained in underway replenishment procedures was the fleet able to be effectively re-supplied at sea. The reason Ltjg. Anderson's ship visited Eniwetok was to replenish its supplies of food and ammunition from a fixed supply point rather than attempt to

replenish at sea. This meant that the ship was not available for action until it returned to its battle fleet south of the Caroline Islands.

Even when food was available in such places as Australia or New Zealand, the shortage of both refrigerated supply ships and refrigerated storage spaces aboard our fighting ships made it necessary for a majority of food supplies to be canned or dehydrated, even though the preservation process used in canning and drying foods destroyed many of the precious nutrients needed by our fighting forces on the front lines. Long supply lines increased the spoilage of fresh foods, and improper storage at supply points throughout the hot and humid Western Pacific resulted in the destruction of food supplies, sometimes on a massive scale. Thus, in many cases, ships returning to rear areas to replenish their food supplies were issued whatever was available instead of what was in the Standard Naval Ration passed by Congress. In many cases, the sailors ate the same rations as Army and Marine units ashore. Many ships were forced to feed their crews canned C Rations because of limited food supplies near the battle lines.

The second factor affecting the quality of the food delivered to the *U.S.S. Key* was a theory that had long been argued among the naval commanders of the various fighting forces. The basis for this theory was that men performing at higher stress levels needed more calories in order to stay alert and able to fight long engagements with the enemy. To sustain their fighting abilities, these men needed to be provided with higher quality foods. As this theory became acknowledged as fact, the rations provided were, in fact, based upon the rigors encountered by the crews assigned to ships performing different duties throughout the various fleets.

Submarine forces received special rations because of the stress encountered by their crews during long, undersea patrols. These special rations were made available to the submarine fleets stationed in either Hawaii or Australia where supply lines were secure and relatively short. But what is not well known is that the admirals responsible for fighting the fleets of carrier aircraft were using the same arguments made by the submarine forces to obtain special food supplies for the crews of their ships and planes.

Prior to the war, naval tactics were centered around battleships and their support ships that the admirals thought would fight battles like those fought in World War I. The attack by the Japanese on December 7, 1941, followed closely by the battles of the Coral Sea and Midway, proved that this new conflict was to be fought in a new way; in the air by squadrons of aircraft. In most cases, the battleships of the opposing forces in this war would never come into the range of one-another's guns. Pilots and crewmen of the aircraft making up the vast air armadas fighting the Japanese in the Pacific and the German U-boat fleet in the Atlantic were in the air for long hours patrolling the vastness of the sea in search of the enemy. Battles were intense and casualties high among both airmen and the men who manned the carrier forces. Because of this, it was decided that rations supplied to carriers and their aircrews should be of the best quality possible to maintain crew efficiency. Thus, ships like the *U.S.S. Keys*, a destroyer escort on duty in the Pacific, would, for now, receive food supplies somewhat inferior to those supplied to the submarine and carrier forces.

A SAMPLE MENU FOR A CREW OF AN AIRCRAFT CARRIER AT SEA MIGHT LOOK LIKE THE FOLLOWING:

BREAKFAST: *Fruit cup, dry cereal, milk (dehydrated or fresh), creamed chipped beef on toast, Danish twists, butter, and coffee.*

DINNER: *Green split pea soup, roast beef with natural gravy, glazed onions, corn, sliced pineapple, bread, butter, and coffee.*

SUPPER: *Pigs in blankets, hashed browned potatoes, berry pie, bread, butter, and coffee. Fresh fruit and mixed salads with dressings would be added for those stationed near a source of fresh food.*

> **AT THE OTHER END OF THE SPECTRUM IS A MENU I RECEIVED FROM A FORMER CREWMAN OF A DESTROYER ESCORT SUCH AS THE *U.S.S. KEYS*:**
>
> **BREAKFAST:** *Pork and beans (canned), bread, and coffee with sugar and condensed milk*
>
> **LUNCH:** *Vegetable beef soup with saltine crackers and coffee with sugar and condensed milk*
>
> **DINNER:** *Sliced luncheon meats, corn bread, tapioca pudding with raisins, and coffee with sugar and condensed milk.*

There were usually condiments such as jam, pickles, syrup, vinegar, ketchup, mustard, salt and pepper available during all meals.

Conditions on the mess decks of our World War II fleets were still much improved when comparing the food provided to our men at sea during this war with that provided the sailors who served at the turn of the century. Much had changed in the galleys of our much-expanded fleet since the *U.S.S. Olympia* set sail from Hong Kong on its way to meet the Spanish fleet in Manila Bay in 1898.

BECAUSE OF THE PROBLEMS ENCOUNTERED IN SUPPLYING FRESH FOOD TO THE FLEET, MANY MENUS WERE BASED ON CANNED VEGETABLES.

Not only had food preparation become centralized and modernized aboard ship, but a new Standard Ration Law was authorized by 10 US Code 6082 in 1933. This law stated that "each person, so entitled, may be served the following quantities of food each day:

- *8 ounces biscuit, or 12 ounces of soft bead, or 12 ounces of flour*
- *12 ounces preserved meat, or 14 ounces salt or smoked meat, or 20 ounces fresh meat or fresh fish or poultry*
- *12 ounces dried vegetables, or 18 ounces canned vegetables, or 44 ounces fresh vegetables*
- *4 ounces dried fruit, or 10 ounces canned fruit, or 6 ounces preserved fruit, or 16 ounces fresh fruit, or 6 ounces canned fruit or vegetable juices, or one ounce powdered fruit juices, or 6-10 ounce concentrated fruit juices*
- *2 ounces cocoa, or 2 ounces coffee, or ½ ounce tea*
- *4 ounces evaporated milk, or 1 ounce powdered milk, or ½ pint fresh milk*
- *1.6 ounces butter*
- *1.6 ounces cereal, rice, or starch foods*
- *1.2 eggs*

- *1.6 ounces lard or lard substitutes*
- *²/₅ gill oils, or sauces, or vinegar*
- *5 ounces sugar*
- *Baking powder and soda, flavoring extracts, mustard,*
  pepper, pickles, salt, syrup, spices and yeast as required."

Although the law stated that a Standard Ration was authorized, one is reminded that in many cases, the exigencies of war dictated more about what supplies were available to a ship's crew than a law passed by the Congress some two or three thousand miles away.

Abandon-ship rations stored aboard a ship's lifeboats and rafts were designated as one pound of hard bread and three-fourths pound of canned meat per man. If a landing party were sent ashore, each man was to be provided with a ration of 2 pounds of hard bread, 2 pounds of canned meat, 8 ounces of sugar, and 4 ounces of coffee in bags.

Special rations were authorized for use by some of the patrol aircraft of the Navy. Unprepared cruising rations, which could be prepared in the aircraft's on-board galley during extended seaplane flights, were as follows:

Meats, individual size, in tins and glass
Soups, canned, in tins
Pickles, sweet, individual size, in tins or glass
Jam or jelly, individual size, in tins or glass
Tomatoes, individual size, in tins
Tomato juice
Cookies
Bar chocolate

Along with this new ration law came a new, much expanded cookbook. Filled with over 500 recipes, it also contained detailed instructions concerning meal planning, the ordering, storage and handling of a wider range of foodstuffs, and expanded instructions for the preparation of fresh, frozen, and canned meats, fruits and vegetables. Cooks were trained in special schools prior to being sent to the fleet. There they learned to use equipment new to the galley such as steam kettles and gas-fired grills that replaced the monster wood or coal-fired stoves that had dominated the galleys of the fleet's ships since the Revolutionary War. Instead of a single, cavernous oven in a single galley stove, banks of electric ovens became the standard aboard newly constructed vessels. This allowed for the roasting of a number of separate entrées at different temperatures at the same time. Cooking staffs grew as training improved. Several new ratings or food service specialties emerged as food preparation became more specialized.

The food services were organized within a separate Commissary Department headed by an officer who received special training in the management of the various messes aboard. The Commissary Officer was responsible for the organization and administration of this department.

The Chief Commissary Steward (CCS) was responsible for the day-to-day operation of the various messes within the Commissary Department. This senior enlisted rating prepared the weekly bill of fare for all messes, estimated the ration components required to support the weekly menu, and provided the Commissary Officer a list of provisions required for each mess on a weekly basis. He was also responsible for the performance of all enlisted men assigned to duties as cooks, stewards, and mess men, as well as the proper preparation and cooking of all foods. This rating was re-designated Chief Commissaryman in 1948.

The Ship's Cook (SC) in charge of the galley was responsible for the actual operation of all activities concerning the preparation and cooking of ship's rations. He was in charge of the galley, bake shop, butcher shop, vegetable and fruit preparation rooms, and the cooking and serving of the food.

The preparation of food for the crew had become so complex that it necessitated two crews working 12-hour shifts. In this case, one or more Ship's cooks was put in charge of a crew called a watch. These lower-ranked petty officers worked under the immediate supervision of the Chief Commissary Steward and the Ship's Cook, and had the responsibilities of mustering the galley crew, directing the cooks and strikers assigned to the watch, and personally supervising the preparation, proper cooking, and serving of all food in an appetizing manner.

A petty officer within the department was assigned duties in the issuing room under the direct supervision of the Chief Commissary Steward (CCS). This person, known as the "Jack of the Dust," was responsible for the receipt, custody, and issue of all commissary department stores entrusted to him. He held the keys to the storerooms and with a crew of lower-rated men, issued the provisions needed by the various messes. (This rating was officially disestablished in 1893, but the informal title continues to be used in the U.S. fleet to this day. The person filling this role is usually an experienced Ship's Cook.)

THE OFFICERS' WARDROOM ON A DESTROYER ESCORT LEFT LITTLE ROOM FOR ANYTHING OTHER THAN THE EATING OF MEALS.

Other ratings included in the newly-expanded Commissary Department included Butchers (SCB), Officer's Cooks (OC), and Stewards (ST), the later two being responsible for the operation of the officers' wardroom as well as the serving of meals there. Various non-rated mess men and strikers were responsible for assisting in the preparation and serving of the food to the crew in the various messes located throughout the ship.

Sailors working in these various ratings either received training at formal schools throughout the shore establishment, or were trained in the fleet using on-the-job training. Rating manuals were published for individual study. As the requirements for more sophisticated methods of food preparation and serving became the new standard in the fleet, the men serving in the various ratings were required to pass fleet-wide rating proficiency examinations in addition to obtaining the recommendation for advancement by their commanding officers.

"Let's take him through the galley and scare the cooks."

Recipes representing this period are taken from two sources.

The Cook Book of the United States Navy, revised in1945, was issued by the Bureau of Supplies and Accounts. This extensive work includes 522 recipes, plus chapters concerning food preparation, sanitation, nutrition, and menu planning. It also contains general information including tables for conversion from dry or wet measure to weight, and for increasing or decreasing the quantitative proportions from the standard recipe set for 100 men to portions for larger or smaller messes. These recipes have precise measurements of all ingredients, and temperature settings for ovens are included. Numerous variations on a particular recipe are offered in order to introduce variety into the crew's menus.

THE CREW CONSTANTLY POKED FUN AT THE COOKS AND THE MEALS THEY HAD TO PRODUCE FROM SOMETIMES LIMITED SUPPLIES.

I include here the conversion formula for messes larger or smaller than 100 as summarized from *The Cook Book of the United States Navy*.

The amount of food necessary for any given mess will vary in accordance with the care of its preparation, the other foods on the menu, the likes and dislikes of the men being fed, the care with which the food is served and the number of men present at each meal. Absenteeism has a direct bearing on the amount of food necessary for the mess. Food should be prepared for the number of men who will be present at mess, not for the number assigned to the mess. For these and other reasons, the amount of issue on a particular item may actually be less than the amount called for in the recipe. In the case where a mess is only serving 64 men, the cook would reduce all ingredients in a recipe to a factor of .64 of that stated in the recipe.

Also, a large mess serving 1000 men will use less food than 10 messes each of 100 men. To conserve food and avoid large amounts of leftovers, the following reductions are recommended: For messes of 500 to 1000 men, first multiply the ingredient measures listed in the basic recipe for 100 men by the appropriate factor reflecting the actual number of men in the mess, (If there are 565 men to be served, the multiplier would be 5.65.) Then reduce the new amounts of ingredients in the recipe by 5 percent. If a recipe calls for one pound of butter for each 100 servings, and the mess is serving 565 men, the actual quantity of butter needed will be determined by first multiplying the one pound by the factor 5.65, which would result in 5.65 pounds reduced by 5 percent, which would result in only 5.37 pounds being used in the recipe.

THE OFFICERS' WARDROOM ON LARGER SHIPS CONTINUED TO BE USED AS A DRESSING STATION FOR BATTLE CASUALTIES DURING WORLD WAR II.

For messes of 1000 or more, multiply by the appropriate factor, and then reduce the new amounts of ingredients in the recipe by 10 percent. (If there are 3,250 men to be served, the multiplier will be 32.5.) For instance, if a recipe calls for one pound of butter for 100 servings, and the crew's mess is serving 3,250 men, the cook will first multiply the one pound by the multiplier 32.5, which equals 32.5 pounds. He will then reduce the result by 10 percent, and use 29.25 pounds in his recipe.

My second source of recipes for this period is *Ship's Cook and Baker,* by Otto Krey, published in 1942. This manual, containing 738 recipes, was written specifically for cooks aboard tankers, cargo, and combination ships. (These ships were operated by members of the Merchant Marine as well as sailors and Marines who manned the ships' weapons.) The quantitative proportions in the recipes in this collection are all calculated for serving messes of 40 persons. These recipes are written in the older fashion of leaving some measurements up to the judgment of the cook. The Introduction of this work contains oven settings and cooking times, in addition to nutritional information and "Practical Cooking Principles."

I have taken great care to copy the recipes exactly as they appear in their original publications in order that my reader may note the changes, not only in cooking practices, but in the written language as well.

THE RECIPES:

Readers may note that the recipes included here have become more sophisticated. The introduction of ovens featuring heat controls into the fleet enabled recipe writers to include oven temperature recommendations matched to separate recipes. One may also note that cooking times have been reduced, thus retaining more of the nutritive value of the foods being prepared.

RECIPES FROM "THE COOK BOOK OF THE UNITED STATES NAVY."

MACARONI REPUBLIC (100-1 CUP PORTIONS)

Ingredients:

- 4 1/2 quarts milk, liquid
- 1 1/2 lb. butter, melted
- 2 pounds pimento, finely chopped
- 10 oz. salt
- 4 oz. pepper
- 1 1/2 tsp. celery salt
- 1 1/2 tsp. mustard, dry
- 3 lbs. cheese, American cheddar, grated
- 36 eggs, beaten
- 4 oz. salt
- 9 gallons water
- 6 lbs. macaroni
- 2 1/4 lbs. bread, cubed
- Paprika to garnish

Instructions:

- Heat milk to boiling temperature. Add butter, pimento, salt, pepper, celery salt and mustard.
- Remove from heat.
- Add cheese, Stir until melted. Add eggs, stirring constantly.
- Add 1/2 cup salt to water. Heat to boiling temperature.
- Stir in macaroni. Cook 20 minutes or until tender. Drain well.
- Combine bread and macaroni. Stir into milk mixture.
- Place in greased baking pans. Sprinkle top with paprika.
- Bake in slow oven (325 degrees F.) about 25 to 30 minutes, or until firm.

Note: The reader may want to compare this recipe with the one for Baked Macaroni in the previous chapter. It is obvious from the ingredients list that sailors who served during World War II had more sophisticated palates than those who had served earlier.

SHRIMP CHOP SUEY (100-1 CUP PORTIONS)

Ingredients:

- 20 lbs. fresh shrimp
- Water to cover
- 1 ½ lbs. pork drippings
- 3 lbs. onions, chopped
- 2 lbs. peppers, green, chopped
- 4 lbs. celery, chopped
- 6 lbs. tomatoes, fresh, cubed
- 1 ½ oz. salt
- ¼ oz. pepper
- 12 lbs. bean sprouts, drained
- 2 gallons fish stock or water
- 1 lb. butter or other fat, melted
- 8 oz. flour
- 1 qt. Soy sauce
- 21 lbs. rice, cooked

Instructions:

- Cover shrimps with water. Heat to boiling temperature.
- Cook 20 minutes. Drain. Plunge into cold water to cool quickly.
- Remove shell. Remove black vein with sharp pointed knife. Wash thoroughly.
- Fry in drippings 10 minutes.
- Add onions, green pepper, celery, tomatoes, salt and pepper. Simmer 10 minutes.
- Add bean sprouts.
- Heat fish stock or water to boiling temperature.
- Blend together fat and flour to a smooth paste. Stir into stock.
- Cook about 10 minutes or until slightly thickened, stirring constantly.
- Stir in Soy sauce. Add sauce to shrimp mixture. Reheat.
- Serve with cooked rice.

Note: 1. 6 No. 5 cans shrimp may be used in place of fresh shrimp.

2. 1 No. 10 can tomatoes may be used in place of fresh tomatoes.

BEAN SOUP (100-1 CUP PORTIONS)

Ingredients:

- 5 ½ lbs. beans, white, dried
- water, cold, to cover
- 5 gals. ham stock
- 1 lb. onions, chopped
- 8 ham bones
- 1 tsp. cloves
- 8 oz. flour
- 1 qt. water, cold
- 2 tsp. pepper
- 4 oz. salt, (if needed)

Instructions:

- Pick over, wash and soak beans, in water to cover, 2 to 3 hours.
- Add ham stock, onions, bones and cloves. Heat to boiling temperature. Let simmer 2 to 3 hours. Remove bones.
- Blend together flour and water to a smooth paste. Stir into soup. Add pepper and salt, if needed.

Note: 1. Ham bones may be omitted.

2. Flour may be omitted. If omitted, the soup must be stirred while serving, as beans will settle to bottom of the container upon standing.

Variation:

BEAN SOUP WITH TOMATOES

- Follow recipe for Bean Soup and add 1 No. 10 can tomatoes to ham stock before simmering.

BEEF STEW (100-1 CUP PORTIONS)

Ingredients:

- 40 lbs. beef, bone in, or 28 lbs. beef boneless
- 6 oz. salt
- 1/2 oz. pepper
- 1 1/2 lbs. flour
- 1 1/2 lbs. fat
- 4 gallons beef stock
- 5 lbs. peas, fresh or frozen
- 12 lbs. tomatoes
- 6 lbs. onions, small quartered
- 6 lbs. carrots, sliced or cubed
- 12 lbs. potatoes, cubed
- 5 lbs. celery, diced
- 1 lb. flour (for gravy)
- 1 1/2 pts. water, cold
- Salt as desired
- Pepper as desired.

Instructions:

- Cut meat into 1 to 2-inch cubes.
- Mix together salt, pepper and flour. Dredge meat in flour. Cook in fat until browned, stirring constantly.
- Add 4 gallons stock or water. Cover. Let simmer 2 1/2 or 3 hours or until tender.
- Cook peas in small amount of water 10 to 15 minutes. Drain.
- Add remaining vegetables to meat mixture. Cook 40 to 45 minutes.
- Blend together flour and water to a smooth paste. Drain stock from meat and thicken with paste.
- Heat to boiling temperature stirring constantly. Add salt and pepper, as desired.

  Pour gravy over meat and vegetables. Reheat. Garnish with cooked peas.

BEEF STEW FOR 2500!

Using the recipe conversion multiplier mentioned in the text of this chapter, we would need to multiply the above recipe for Beef Stew, by a multiplier of 25. We would then reduce our results for each ingredient by 10 percent to account for the number of men who will actually be served. (Remember, not every man aboard would eat every meal served.) I have converted the ingredients for the recipe as follows:

Ingredients:

- 630 lbs. beef, boneless
- 8.5 lbs. salt
- 11.25 oz. pepper
- 33.75 lbs. flour
- 33.75 lbs. fat
- 90 gal. beef stock
- 112.5 lbs. peas, fresh or frozen
- 270 lbs. tomatoes

- 135 lbs. onions, small quartered
- 135 lbs. carrots, sliced or cubed
- 270 lbs. potatoes, cubed
- 112.5 lbs. celery, diced
- 22.5 lbs. flour (for gravy)
- 4.25 gal. water, cold
- Salt as desired
- Pepper as desired

Note: The method for cooking would be similar to above (for Beef Stew) except for cooking times which would have been lengthened.

BAKED CHICKEN AND NOODLES (100-6 OUNCE PORTIONS)

Ingredients:

– 3 oz. salt

– 5 gallons water, boiling

– 7 lbs. noodles

– 2 lbs. chicken or other fat

– 2 lbs. flour

– 4 oz. salt

– 1/2 oz. pepper

– 2 1/2 gals. chicken stock, boiling

– 9 egg yolks

– 10 lbs. chicken (fowl), cooked, diced

– 12 oz. bread crumbs, fine

– 8 oz. butter, melted

Instructions:

– Add 3 oz. salt to water. Heat to boiling temperature. Stir in noodles. Cook about 20 minutes or until tender. Drain.

– Blend together fat, flour, 4 oz. salt and pepper to a smooth paste. Stir in stock. Heat to boiling temperature. Cook, stirring constantly, until thickened.

– Add egg yolks, stirring constantly. Pour sauce over noodles. Stir in chicken. Place in greased baking pans.

– Blend together crumbs and butter. Sprinkle over creamed mixture.

– Bake in hot oven (400 degrees F.) 30 minutes.

Note: Egg yolks may be omitted.

SIMMERED CABBAGE USING DEHYDRATED CABBAGE (100-3 ½oz. PORTIONS)

Ingredients:

– 2 ¾ lbs. cabbage, dehydrated
– 3 gals. water
– 3 oz. salt
– 2 ¼ lbs. bacon, diced
– 1 ⅓ tablespoons pepper

Instructions:

– Soak cabbage in water 45 to 60 minutes. Cover.
– Heat slowly to boiling temperature, about 40 minutes. Add salt. Simmer 10 to 15 minutes.
– Drain ½ the liquid from cabbage and reserve for soups or stews.
– Fry bacon until lightly browned.
– Add bacon, bacon fat and pepper to cabbage. Reheat.

  Note: 1. *1 lb. dehydrated cabbage is equivalent to 16 lbs. fresh cabbage, or to 8 ½ lbs cooked, drained cabbage.*

  2. *Reconstituted cabbage may be used as an ingredient for soups and stews.*

  3. *Dehydrated cabbage must be held in an air-tight container at all times. Absorption of too much moisture will result in development of unsatisfactory flavor.*

CORNED BEEF AND CABBAGE

– Soak and cook cabbage as for Simmered Cabbage, omitting bacon. Drain.
– Add 6 lbs. canned corned beef, broken into small pieces. Mix well. Reheat.

FRENCH FRIED CARROTS

– Clean and cut carrots in strips.
– Cook carrots. Cool. Dip in egg wash. Cover with crumbs.
– Fry in hot deep fat at 375 degrees F. 5 to 7 minutes.

ESCALLOPED POTATOES (100-2/3 C. PORTIONS)

Ingredients:

– 44 lbs. potatoes
– 2 1/2 oz. salt
– 2 1/2 gals.
  Cream Sauce

Instructions:

– Peel and wash potatoes. Slice thin and season with salt.
– Arrange alternate layers of cream sauce and potatoes in greased baking pans. Bottom and top layers should be cream sauce.
– Bake in slow oven (325 degree F.) about 1 1/2 to 2 hours or until potatoes are tender.

  Note: 1. *Finely diced, cooked bacon or ham, green peppers, pimentos or chives may be added to the Cream Sauce.*

  2. *Grated cheese or buttered crumbs may be sprinkled over the top 5 to 10 minutes before removing from oven.*

MEDIUM THICK CREAM OR WHITE SAUCE FOR ESCALLOPED DISHES (100-2 OZ. PORTIONS)

Ingredients:

– 2 lbs. butter or other fat, melted
– 1 lb. flour
– 2 gals. milk, liquid, hot
– 5 Tbs. salt
– 4 tsp. pepper

Instructions:

– Blend fat and flour to a smooth paste. Stir rapidly into hot milk. Cook until thickened. Stir constantly. Add salt and pepper.

BREAD PUDDING (100 1/2 CUP PORTIONS)

I include this recipe so my reader may compare it to the DUFF recipes in previous chapters.

Ingredients:

– 3 gals. milk, liquid
– 5 lbs. bread cubes
– 5 lbs. sugar
– 1 lb. butter or shortening, melted
– 20 eggs, beaten lightly
– 6 Tbs. salt
– 1/4 C. vanilla

Instructions:

– Mix all ingredients together thoroughly.
– Pour into greased baking pans 2 to 2 1/2 inches deep.
– Bake in moderate oven (375 degrees F.) about 1 hour.

  Note: 8 oz. powdered eggs and 1 1/2 pts. water may be used in place of fresh eggs.

RECIPES FROM "SHIP'S COOK AND BAKER."

The reader may note that these recipes appear to be somewhat "tastier" than those served to the sailors aboard combatant ships.

BEEF POT ROAST (40 PORTIONS)

Ingredients:

– 25 lb. meat
– 7 pieces fat bacon
– Salt
– 40 peppercorns
– 7 bay leaves
– 7 cloves
– 1 C. suet
– 1 C. flour
– 3 onions
– Water

Instructions:

– The meat - from the rump, chuck or sirloin - is pounded. The bacon, cut in small thick pieces, is stuck into the meat. Heat the suet, add the onions, and brown the meat slightly on both sides.

– Brown the flour in the suet, add water and the spices, and cook. Put the browned meat into the gravy, which should cover it. Cover the pot well (an iron pot is best). Put the covered roast into a moderately hot oven from 2 1/2 to 3 hrs., basting frequently.

– Take the roast out when done, and prepare the gravy. Take off all fat; if too thick, add more water; strain.

HAMBURG STEAK, GERMAN STYLE (40 PORTIONS)

Ingredients:

– 16 lb. chopped steak
– 7 Tbs. butter
– 8 eggs
– 7 tsp. grated onion
– 3/4 lb. butter or lard
– Salt and pepper

Instructions:

– Lean meat from the round is chopped or ground fine by putting it through the grinder two or three times. Season and mix with the eggs, butter and onion (omit latter if not desired).

– After mixing well, form scant 1/4 lb. dumplings, flattened to 1 1/2 in. thick. Heat the butter or lard, put in the steaks, and fry about 10 min., turning and basting frequently. Serve the steaks on a hot platter. For gravy, pour a little water into the frying pan with the steak juices, bring to a boil, and pour over the steaks.

– The gravy may be made by adding to the steak butter 3 tbsp. of mustard, 1 tbsp. of flour, and some bouillon or water. Boil 2 min., and strain.

PORK CUTLETS, ROASTED (40 PORTIONS)

Although the title of this recipe calls for roasting, the cutlets are actually fried.

Ingredients:

– 20 lb. pork cutlets
– 7 eggs
– 10 tablespoons milk
– 10 C. grated rolls or white bread
– 7 Tbs. flour
– 7 cloves
– 3 bay leaves
– 1 1/2 small onions
– 4 lb. butter or lard
– 7 C. water
– Salt and pepper

Instructions:

– The cutlets are pounded and seasoned. The eggs are beaten with the milk, the cutlets dipped into this and then into the bread crumbs, then fried until light brown in hot butter or lard. This will require 15 min., if they are 1/2 in. thick; if they are thicker, fry 20 min., and place on a hot platter.

– If there is much fat in the pan, take some of it out; brown onion slices and flour in remaining fat; add water, cloves and bay leaves, also salt and pepper, if necessary, and cook 5 min. Strain and pour over cutlets or serve separately.

STUFFED PEPPERS (40 PORTIONS)

Ingredients:

– 40 sweet peppers
– 1 qt. crumbs
– 1/8 C. chopped onion
– 1 qt. minced veal, chicken, or other cooked meat
– 3/4 tsp. pepper
– Stock (or tomato juice or soup)
– Salt

Instructions:

– Wash and cut the peppers in two; remove seeds and tough white portions. Wash and cook in boiling water 5 min., or in a steamer 5 to 8 min. Mix the other ingredients and add stock, tomato juice, or tomato soup to moisten. Fill the peppers with the mixture, and bake at 400 degrees F. for 15 to 20 min.

HEADCHEESE OF CALF'S TONGUE AND PIG'S FEET (40 PORTIONS)

This recipe makes me feel like we have stepped back into the 19th century again.

Ingredients:

– 30 pig's feet
– 12 calves' tongues
– Juice of 3 lemons
– 10 Tbs. vinegar
– Salt
– 3 small onions
– 3 sour pickles, cut into small pieces
– 12 qt. water
– 1 tsp. pickle spices

Instructions:

– Once the pig's feet and calves' tongues are cleaned well, put on to boil in water, with salt, pepper, onions, bay leaves. Cover the pot and cook until well done. Then skin the tongue, and cut it and the rest of the meat into small pieces.

– Strain the bouillon, and add the vinegar and lemon juice. Put the meat into a dish and pour the bouillon over it, and set to cool. Then turn it out onto a platter, and serve with head lettuce or potato salad and vinegar and oil or Mayonnaise Dressing, or with fried potatoes.

ESCALLOPED EGGS WITH HAM (40 PORTIONS)

Ingredients:

- 80 eggs
- 3/8 lb. milk
- 1 1/2 lb. flour
- 3/8 lb. crackers
- 4 lb. ham, boiled and chopped fine
- 3/8 lb. butter
- Salt and pepper to taste

Instructions:

- Boil the eggs hard, shell and cut them into quarters or eights. Place the butter and flour in a clean pan. Make a white roux, and reduce this with hot water to the desired thickness. Season to taste, remove from fire; when partly cooled, add the milk. Now pour a little of the sauce into clean baking pans, arrange a layer of eggs, a layer of chopped ham, and a layer of cracker crumbs. Repeat this until pans are filled. Dot each with a little butter. Bake in a medium oven for about 15 min., or until browned.

PARKER HOUSE ROLLS (40 PORTIONS)

Ingredients:

- 3 1/2 lb. flour
- 1 1/2 qt. scalded milk
- 1 C. butter
- 6 tsp. sugar
- 3 eggs
- 3 tsp. salt
- 4 oz. compressed yeast
- 1 C. lukewarm water

Instructions:

- Add the butter, sugar, and salt to the milk; when warm, add the yeast, dissolved in lukewarm water. Add the eggs, slightly beaten. Stir in the flour gradually, and form into a soft dough, adding (if desired) 4 large freshly cooked riced potatoes, and only enough more flour to knead. Cover, and let rise in a warm place until double its bulk.

- Toss gently on a floured board, handling as little as possible.

- Pat or roll the dough 1/3 in. thick, brush well with melted butter, cut into rounds 2 1/2 in. across. Fold over double with edges meeting. Press a finger through the center edges to fix the shape. Place in rows close together in greased pans. Allow to stand until slightly raised, then bake in hot oven (450 degrees F.) 12 to 15 min., decreasing the heat.

GUMBO SOUP (40 PORTIONS)

Ingredients:

- 5 gal. chicken stock
- 1 lb. ham fat
- 1 lb. carrots
- 1 lb. rice
- 3/4 lb. okra
- 2 lb. veal shanks
- 1 lb. onions
- 1/4 lb. butter
- 1 1/2 lb. tomatoes

Instructions:

- If stock is not prepared, cut three full-grown chickens into halves. Put them into pot with veal, adding a little salt; cover with cold water, and place on fire. When it begins to boil, add the ham fat, onions, and carrots, minced fine and fried in butter. Simmer 2 hrs., or until chickens are tender. Remove the chickens. When soup cools, skim off all fat, add the tomatoes, okra, and rice, and simmer 1 hr. longer. Season with salt and pepper.

STRAWBERRY CHIFFON PIE (40 PORTIONS)

Ingredients:

- 10 Tbs. gelatin
- 1 1/4 C. cold water
- 10 pt. fresh strawberries, crushed
- 10 C. sugar
- 1 1/2 C. lemon juice
- 6 tsp. salt
- 10 egg whites
- 10 C. heavy cream (or canned milk), whipped

Instructions:

- Soften the gelatin in cold water, and dissolve over hot water. Combine the crushed strawberries, sugar, lemon juice, and salt. Add the gelatin mixture and chill until slightly thickened. Beat the egg whites until stiff and fold in the whipped cream. Fold in the strawberry mixture. Pile lightly into baked pie shells. Chill in the refrigerator several hours, or until firm.

BAKED PIE SHELLS

Ingredients:

- 5 lb. flour
- 4 lb. shortening
- 1 qt. water, cold
- 5 oz. sugar
- 2 1/2 oz salt

Instructions:

- Mix all the dry ingredients thoroughly with the shortening, until the mixture becomes course and granular in appearance. Now add the water, and work in lightly until the dough just holds together.
- Roll out the dough and cut into pieces large enough to fit each pie pan, leaving some dough to hang over the edges. Crimp the dough at the edges, and perforate bottoms to allow escape of steam. Bake in hot oven (425-450 degrees F.) for 10 to 15 min. Let cool before using.

APPLE CAKE, DUTCH (40 PORTIONS)

Ingredients:

- 3 lb. sifted flour
- 6 tsp. baking powder
- 3 lb. sugar
- 1 Tbs. salt
- 1 C. shortening
- 6 eggs, well beaten
- 4 C. milk
- 1 C. shortening
- 6 Tbs. butter
- 4 C. brown sugar (firmly packed)
- 1 gal. apples, sliced
- 1/4 oz. cinnamon

Instructions:

- Sift flour with baking powder, sugar, and salt. Cut in the shortening until the mixture is as fine as meal. Combine the beaten egg and milk, and add to flour mixture, mixing to a soft dough.
- Melt 1 C. shortening and the butter together; add the brown sugar, cinnamon, and salt, and mix well; pour into 16 X 16 in. pans, greased with shortening. Press the apple slices in a circle over this. Spread the dough over apples. Bake in a moderate oven (350 degrees F.) 50 to 60 min. Bake with the pans in normal position-i.e., with the apples on the bottom, so that they will bake tender. To serve, reverse the pan in turning out, so the apples are on top.

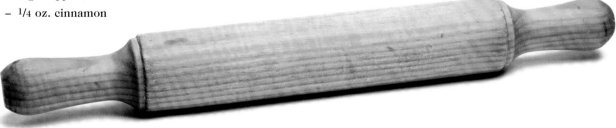

Chapter 5

ALMOST AS GOOD AS MOM USED TO MAKE

Cooking for a Modern Navy

ABOARD THE ATTACK AIRCRAFT CARRIER *U.S.S. Coral Sea* on Yankee Station off the coast of Vietnam in 1967, Commissaryman First Class Charlie Kiefer had one last duty to complete before crawling into his bunk located in a compartment just below the main galley. Charlie had never been so tired. His body ached from his shoulder blades to the backs of his thighs. Although every bone in his body screamed out for sleep, Charlie had to write a letter to his wife, Diana, to let her know he was all right and not to worry after the news about what had happened aboard his ship got back to the States and the folks back home.

Charlie had entered the U.S. Navy in 1956, and his first ship was a destroyer. Like many others who didn't do well on the entry examinations administered by the navy during boot camp training, Charlie didn't qualify for any specialty training. Sent directly to the fleet, he served at the convenience of the naval service in whatever capacity he was needed. After checking into the deck division aboard his first command, he was informed that he would have to serve his first three months aboard as a Mess Cook helping out in the ship's galley before he could join the rest of the crew and begin learning his trade as a Boatswain's Mate.

Unlike the earlier years when each mess had consisted of from 8 to 30 men fed by an unskilled seaman, the modern Navy now fed its enlisted crew members from a centrally located general mess staffed by trained cooks and bakers. Centralization of messing facilities was complete by the end of the Second World War. In the newly organized mess, men sent to the galley by each division on a rotating basis augmented the number of trained cooks assigned to perform the tasks necessary to feed the crew. These men, known as Mess Cooks, assisted in food preparation, cooking, serving and cleaning the equipment in the area where the food was served. While serving in what many others usually considered arduous duty, Charlie found his purpose in life. He enjoyed working in the galley so much that he approached the Leading Petty Officer and requested a permanent transfer to the S2 Division that was responsible for the feeding of the enlisted men aboard.

COOKS IN THE
MODERN NAVY
EMPLOY THE SAME
EQUIPMENT USED
BY CHEFS IN
BLUE RIBBON
RESTAURANTS
ASHORE.

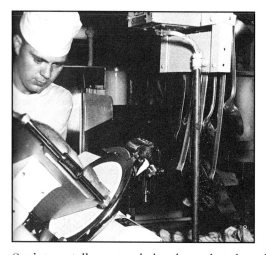

During his career in the Navy, Charlie served aboard another destroyer, a cruiser, and an aviation squadron. He became a designated Commissaryman Striker, with an entry in his record that he was now to be assigned directly to the galley crew when serving aboard any naval vessel or station. He advanced through the ranks from Commissaryman Third Class to the rank of First Class Petty Officer. By 1967 he was serving as the Watch Captain of the starboard watch , with the responsibility of overseeing the smooth operation of the *U.S.S. Coral Sea's* two galleys, two bake shops, butcher shop and vegetable preparation room during the 2000 to 0800 watch.

Unlike most surface ships that serve morning, mid-day, and evening meals at set times throughout the day, aircraft carriers operate their messing facilities 24 hours a day. Normal flight operations are conducted around the clock so the crew needs to be fed on a continuing basis. Having two galleys to feed the crew allows the ship's cooks to feed both the day and night watches, thus enabling the crew to maintain the high state of readiness necessary for sustained 24 hour a day operations.

IT TAKES MASSIVE
QUANTITIES OF
PROVISIONS TO
PRODUCE THE
13,000+ MEALS
NEEDED EACH DAY
TO FEED THE
HUNGRY CREW OF
AN AIRCRAFT
CARRIER.

Charlie Kiefer's assignment aboard the *U.S.S. Coral Sea* placed him among those at the top of the leadership ladder in his division which was responsible for the proper feeding of a ship's crew of some 4500 men in accordance with the guidelines set out by the Chief of Naval Personnel and the Subsistence Division of the Bureau of Supplies and Accounts. In the modern navy, men like Charlie conducted their duties in accordance with the guidance received from volumes of instructions dictating every aspect of food preparation from the purchasing and inspection of provisions to the disposal of the waste products that resulted from their preparation and consumption. Every man assigned to the ship's galley received both formal and informal training. Unlike their predecessors who had been left pretty much to their own devices while preparing the food for their respective messes, the modern day navy cook's day-to-day performance

TODAY, CULINARY SPECIALISTS FOLLOW STANDARDIZED RECIPES THAT ENSURE CONSISTENTLY HIGH-QUALITY MEALS THROUGHOUT THE FLEET.

was observed, evaluated, and corrected as necessary by a cadre of officers, chief petty officers and leading petty officers who had received extensive training in formal classrooms in naval establishments both ashore and afloat. Training manuals were written and distributed to the crewmen for self-study in preparation for in-depth examinations concerning both the practical skills necessary for proper food preparation as well as the leadership skills necessary to manage galley crews. Successful completion of these examinations meant advancement in both rank and responsibility.

By the time Charlie Kiefer reached his position aboard the *U.S.S. Coral Sea*, he was entrusted with the management of a staff of some 18 men responsible for the preparation and serving of the crew's midnight rations at 2300, breakfast at 0400, and the preparation of the mid-day meal for serving at 1000. In addition to these duties, Charlie was responsible for the baking of all rolls, breads, muffins, pies, cakes, and pastries to be served within the next 24 hours. His vegetable shop personnel were busy preparing all of the vegetables to be served during the next watch, from peeling potatoes and carrots for tomorrow's beef stew, to preparing canned and fresh fruit and salads that were always available to the men passing through the ship's food service lines. His butcher was busy defrosting, cutting and trimming the various meats and poultry that would be used in the preparation of the menus developed by the S2 Division Chief Petty Officer and approved by the S2 Division Officer and the Executive Officer. The recipes for these menus had been delivered to the Watch Captain's desk located just off the galley during the day watch and were ready for Charlie when he came on watch at 2000.

But Charley's last watch aboard the *U.S.S. Coral Sea* on Yankee Station in the Gulf of Tonkin had been different.

The night watch in the aft galley started out as usual. Charlie always arrived at least thirty minutes early to ensure a smooth turnover between the day and night crews. It had been eighteen days since the ship completed its last refit and crew rest in the Philippines, and the crew had settled into the rhythm of a fighting ship at sea: working, eating, more working, and sleeping if you could find the time. The ship had been conducting around-the-clock flight operations for the past three days, and although there were no easy days in a galley responsible for serving over 12,000 meals a day, the turn-over from the day crew was smooth, and in no time Charlie's crew began preparations for serving Mid-Rats for the night crew. Mid-Rats consisted of leftovers from the day's lunch and dinner, as well as eggs and omelets to order and some form of breakfast meat. This helped to reduce the amount of food wasted as well as provide the night crews some of the most interesting meals served aboard ship. It was not unusual for a sailor to pass along the serving line during Mid-Rats and have his pick of fried chicken, meat loaf, and roast beef, plus ham and eggs with all of the trimmings. This meal was so popular with the crew that some members of the day watch would get out of their bunks to go to Mid-Rats so they could have another helping of a particularly good meal served earlier in the day.

Almost immediately after assuming the watch at 2000, the General Quarters Alarm sounded throughout the ship, followed by the trill of the Boatswain's Mate of the Watch's pipe and the call, "GENERAL QUARTERS, GENERAL QUARTERS! ALL HANDS MAN

YOUR BATTLE STATIONS! GENERAL QUARTERS, GENERAL QUARTERS! THIS IS NOT A DRILL!"

The men assigned to the night watch in the galley were assigned General Quarters stations either in the compartment containing the galley, or at stations close by. After manning their stations and dogging down the hatches to seal off the compartment, Charlie and his men stood by to follow whatever orders came over the communications circuits that connected them to the rest of the ship. Ventilation ducts were closed to ensure the watertight integrity of the space, and it wasn't long before the heat from the ovens, now shut off, raised the temperature to an uncomfortable level. Soon a telephone talker reported that a Zuni Rocket being assembled on the forward mess deck had exploded killing two Ordnancemen. The mess decks of aircraft carriers are multi-purpose areas. Not only are the men served their meals there, the spaces are also used for weapons assembly and damage control, as well as triage stations by the ship's medical staff. The forward mess deck, closed at night, was being used by the ship's Weapons Department to assemble bombs and rockets needed for the night's launches. Somehow one of these weapons exploded and another live rocket was wedged against a bulkhead and could explode at any moment. Charlie's team were told to stand by for further orders, so he set his men to work doing what they could to prepare for the feeding of the crew after General Quarters was over.

At 2200, the phone talker received the order from Damage Control Central for all the men in the aft galley to report to the forward galley to assist in the passing of ammunition out of the space so it could be thrown over the side, thus reducing the chance of further damage should the rocket wedged against the bulkhead explode. Charlie and his crew reported as ordered and soon formed a chain of men pushing or passing bombs and rocket components out of the forward mess deck to the hangar deck where other men threw them over the side into the ocean.

Charlie's team was then assigned to the Aircraft Handler's crew to assist in pushing aircraft out of the forward hangar bay to protect them in case there was an explosion on the deck below. After securing as many aircraft as possible, Charlie and his crew were assigned to the aft hangar bay where they were given the job of securing ammunition staged there that was now rolling freely on the deck as the ship, now almost dead in the water, rolled in the sea's swells.

It took the EOD (Explosive Ordinance Disposal) Officer more than eight hours to disable the rocket and end the crisis aboard the ship. By the time the ship secured from General Quarters, more than 16 hours had

FOOD SERVICE ATTENDANTS ASSIST TRAINED STAFF MEMBERS BY MAKING SURE ALL COOKING IMPLEMENTS ARE CLEAN AND READY FOR USE WHEN NEEDED.

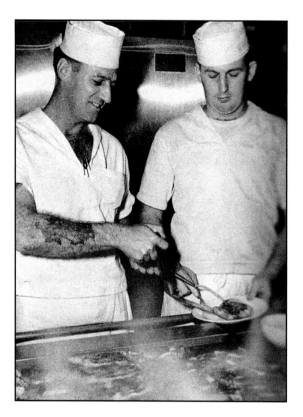

passed and it was 1200 (noon) of the day following the explosion forward.

Now Charlie was faced with another problem: the ship's crew had not had anything to eat in over 20 hours and Charlie and his crew were due to begin their next 12-hour watch at 2000. Charlie led his crew aft to the galley and met the Watch Captain from the day crew. After a short conference, a decision was made to mobilize their combined crews and light off every oven and grill in the galley. For the next 24 hours the two teams provided the ship's crew with continuous meals which they prepared using all the available meats and vegetables on the ship.

Now, in the early hours of his third day of continuous duty, Charley was tired; bone tired. Setting pen to paper, he wrote out a short letter filled with assurances that he was well, and that he loved his wife and children dearly. Then he crawled into his bunk, not even bothering to strip off his dirty clothes, and slept soundly until he was called to duty again as Watch Captain of the *U.S.S. Coral Sea's* 2000 to 0800 Main Galley Watch.

I believe it is appropriate to mention here that neither Charlie, nor any other member of his watch, received any special recognition for their participation in this true event aboard the *U.S.S. Coral Sea*. No medals were awarded his crew, no special entries were made in their personnel records. Nothing was said beyond the personal acknowledgement given his team by his Division Officer and Chief Petty Officer, and the thanks to the crew given by their grateful skipper during the following days. Charlie and his crew had acted as expected: serving as ordered to serve; going into harm's way without any thought of personal safety: doing the job that needed to be done in order to save their fellow crew members and their ship. But Charlie and his crew didn't have to go that extra mile by serving hot food to an exhausted crew through the 24 hours following the explosion in the forward mess decks. This was a matter of personal commitment to his fellow shipmates and his ship. It is this commitment to their fellow blue jackets, that makes every man and woman serving aboard ships in our nation's navy a special breed.

Aircraft carriers like the *U.S.S. Midway* and the *U.S.S. Coral Sea* had two galleys, one or the other of which was open 23 hours a day. The main galley, located on the mess deck aft, was the larger of the two and served traditional meals three times a day. The smaller, forward galley prepared donuts that were issued to the various coffee messes located in divisional spaces throughout the ship (a remnant of the early day navy's messing system). Another function of the forward mess was to provide fast food meals for crew members who did not choose to stand in the longer mess lines aft, or had read the menu for a particular meal and chose to eat the hot dogs and hamburgers served with chili and fries. This galley closed after the evening meal and then became either a recreation area for the crew or a weapons handling space.

The exigencies of almost continuous on-going foreign commitments resulted in technological breakthroughs in food preparation as well as ship and weapons design in the U.S. Navy. Since the Vietnam War, improvements in the grills used in the preparation of fried foods changed from gas-fired grills to electrically heated units. Ovens with sophisticated temperature controls resulted in more tender roasts and cuts such as baked hams and roasted turkeys. Deep fat fryers were introduced into the fleet making

THE MESS DECKS ON AIRCRAFT CARRIERS ARE SO CROWDED THAT CREWMEN HAVE TO WAIT FOR THEIR SHIPMATES TO FINISH EATING BEFORE THEY CAN FIND A PLACE TO SIT.

RATING BADGE
WORN BY
COMMISSARYMEN.

it possible to replicate things like French fries and fish and chips that the sailors were used to consuming ashore. Additional seasonings were made available on a large scale so navy cooks could dress up their menu items to suit the particular tastes of the crews. Mexican, Italian, and Oriental food nights became common aboard ship. Fruits and vegetables were given extended storage life by the introduction of Ethylene absorption blankets in chill boxes. These blankets absorb the ethylene gas emitted by fresh fruits and vegetables that in turn causes them to rot.

Today's navy uses equipment unheard of aboard Charlie's ship in 1967. Galleys are equipped with such devices as Combination Ovens, Clam Shell Grills, the Skittle, and the Condiment Dispenser to name just a few. Each of these pieces of equipment has resulted in an increase in the number of food items offered by the galley as well as a decrease in preparation and clean up times.

New food items introduced to improve a sailor's repast while at sea include cold storage eggs. This process extends the shelf life of the egg to as much as 90 days. Powdered eggs have become a thing of the past, even in scrambled eggs. They are now relegated to the bakeshop where they are included in premixed containers requiring a minimum of mixing. Omelets and scrambled eggs make use of frozen eggs that have been broken and mixed before freezing. "Bug Juice," or powdered drink mixes common on the mess decks for so many years, have been replaced with fountain drink machines, now referred to by today's Mess Management Specialists as "Bag in a Box." Today's sailors can now serve themselves fountain drinks, juices, tea or various flavored ades just like the ones offered in fast food restaurants ashore.

No longer are butchers needed to cut up sides or quarters of beef, pork, chicken, or lamb in preparation for cooking. Chill rooms are now stocked with meats prepared in roast, steak, and patty form that move directly from the packing box to the cooking tray. Pre-breaded pork chops, veal steaks and other specialty foods such as boneless, skinless chicken breasts produce healthier meals, which are prepared with reduced amounts of salt. Dehydrated, compressed foods, have improved greatly over those early concoctions introduced during the Civil War. Now dehydrated pork chops, peas, green beans, soups, and even cottage cheese are used in navy galleys fleet wide. Efforts by senior officers in the Medical Corps have resulted in less fat, more fiber, and a tripling of the fruit and vegetable consumption in the enlisted mess. Pre-cooked food items have found their way into the menu of even the smallest naval ship. Precooked bacon, meat patties, deep fried chicken, vegetable and beef lasagna, and frozen dough are now available to menu planners afloat. Items prepared using cook/freeze methods are purchased from contractors ashore. Items currently available include bakery products, soups, gravies, pre-made salads (i.e. macaroni salad), Salisbury steak and meat loaf.

In 1998, Congress changed the Ration Law to set a Basic Allowance for Subsistence (BAS) for each man and woman in the armed forces at $7.98 per day. Supply Officers aboard individual ships are allowed to use these amounts in determining menu content for the crew. This amount may be supplemented based upon operational schedules and special environmental conditions such as extreme heat or cold. Officers continue to pay for their food on a personal basis. The Wardroom Mess charges each officer the same $7.98 per day, plus an additional $50.00 per month to cover the costs of his or her meals. Because the BAS is paid directly to the officers instead of to the ship's supply officer, individual officers pay their mess bills monthly in accordance with the number of days they are aboard ship and the number of meals consumed. Of particular note is that although the officers are paying more, the quality of the food in the Wardroom is no better than that being consumed on the mess decks. Chief petty officers who mess separately from both commissioned officers and other enlisted ranks, may choose to pay additional funds to their mess manager in order to have menus sometimes superior to both officer and enlisted. During my years of active duty from 1957 to 1976, it was not unusual to see fish and chips served on the mess decks, the officers consuming

AS REQUIRED BY NAVAL REGULATIONS, THE OFFICER OF THE DECK (BEHIND POLE AT LEFT) MUST SAMPLE THE FOOD SERVED TO THE CREW EVERY DAY.

baked Pollack filets, while the ship's chiefs were eating steak and lobster. I am told that this tradition has almost disappeared from our modern-day navy.

Not only have menus changed since the Vietnam Era, but the entire system of menu planning has changed. During the early post-World War years, navy cooks were left to their own ingenuity in creating menus using the official *Cook Book of the United States Navy.* Chief Commissarymen and S2 Division Officers tasked with the job of

feeding the crew spread their funds over each month to allow for a sequence of varying wholesome meals on a day-to-day basis, and at the same time holding back funds for special dinners on Thanksgiving, Christmas, or special steak nights. This process could tax both the creativeness and budgets of those involved. As a result of research conducted in special centers studying habitability issues afloat, psychologists determined that people have somewhat limited food memories. As it appears that none of us can remember what we had to eat as little as four to five weeks ago, the navy has developed a standardized menu that covers three meals a day for a period of five weeks. This menu is repeated every five weeks in all the messes aboard ship, whether they be in the wardroom, the CPO Mess, or the crew's galley with the exception of special meals approved by the ship's Executive Officer. I am told, however, that this has enabled the Navy to reduce the number of food items stocked aboard its ships, further reducing costs, which in turn has resulted in more funds being made available for improved individual food items.

UNDERWAY REPLENISHMENT IS A DANGEROUS, WORK-INTENSIVE EVOLUTION INVOLVING MOST OF A SHIP'S CREW.

In 2004, the navy changed the name of its Mess Management Specialists, (MS) to Culinary Specialists (CS) in order to more clearly define the duties of the men and women who manage the cooking, baking, dining and living areas of the ship. Some of today's Culinary Specialists are trained in much the same manner as Charlie Kiefer was a half-century ago. Personnel who are not selected for special training in schools staffed by both civilian chefs and naval personnel are still trained through a system of on-the-job-training and personal study under the watchful eyes of senior petty officers. Others who are selected during their basic training or who have already served a tour of duty in the fleet are sent to advanced training schools where they study under renowned chefs from the American Culinary Institute as well as experienced senior enlisted specialists. Special advanced mobile teams known as Navy Food Management Teams, (NFMTs) travel throughout the fleet, coming aboard for a period of a few days to as long as a week to train shipboard personnel in such areas as nutrition, sanitation, food inspection, food production, and record keeping.

Each year, more than 150 personnel serving in outstanding galleys afloat and ashore, as determined by the Ney Program (introduced into the fleet by Captain Ney, U.S. Navy Supply Corps in 1958, to improve the quality of food in enlisted messes) are invited to attend a 10-day culinary excellence course at the prestigious Culinary Institute of America where they receive training from master and executive chefs.

But the Navy is a very tradition-bound service. Today we can still see remnants of those early years when messes were served by unskilled sailors responsible for feeding a ship's crew. Food Service Attendants, young men and women serving their first year of military service in the fleet, still have to perform duties on the mess decks assisting those who are preparing the crew's meals. As there is only one Culinary Specialist for every 100 personnel aboard ship, an additional three to four persons from each division or squadron are needed to perform all the duties necessary for the preparation of high quality meals. These young men and women are managed by the Mess Deck Master at Arms, a senior enlisted rating responsible for the orderly operation of the mess decks. Among the Food Service Attendants' duties are the cleaning of kitchen utensils; running the scullery where the food trays, glasses, cups and utensils used by the crew are cleaned; keeping the mess deck clean by scrubbing down the tables, benches, chairs and decks; assisting in the serving of food; performing duties as assigned by the cooks in the area of food preparation; making coffee; and keeping the vending, condiment dispensers, and milk machines serviced. They are also responsible for waste management, such as processing trash for food service pulpers, plastic, glass and can processors, the grinding of food waste, and the storage of grease in 55-gallon drums which are stored until the ship returns to shore.

The recipes I have chosen for this chapter range from the mundane to the exotic. Most are contained in the standard menu currently being used in the U.S. Navy. I have included menu items from all three meals normally served aboard a ship at sea as well as desserts, and side dishes. I have presented the recipes as they are cataloged in the official Armed Forces Recipe Service that contains over 1500 tested recipes yielding

SENIOR ENLISTED
MEN, SUCH AS THIS
MASTER CHIEF
PETTY OFFICER,
ARE RESPONSIBLE
FOR MAINTAINING
ADEQUATE
INVENTORIES TO
ENSURE NECESSARY
INGREDIENTS ARE
AVAILABLE WHEN
REQUIRED.

100 portions printed on 5-by 8-inch cards. These cards are used in the galley, sometimes hung from clips over workstations such as mixing tables and steam kettles.

As in the previous chapter, those preparing the meals are required to modify the recipes to reflect the number of persons actually being served during each meal. The multipliers and reducers mentioned in the previous chapter continue to apply to the preparation of the recipes that follow. Increased complexity of the recipes required additional information to be provided. First, is wet and dry measure. New recipe cards now include quantities listed both in weights such as pounds and ounces and measures such as quarts, cups, tablespoons, and portions of teaspoons.

Secondly, is the difference between the purchased quantity and the edible portion remaining to be consumed. This is especially important when serving fruits and vegetables canned in liquids. Recipes using fresh fruits such as pineapples or bananas also need to reflect actual edible weights verses unprepared weights. Thus, some recipes denote both A.P., or "As Purchased" weights, as well as E.P., "Edible Portions".

The recipe cards are indexed using a letter and number sequence. The letters run from A, which contains General Information, through Q, Vegetables. A section containing 44 vegetarian recipes follows the last letter.

MORE COMPLEX MENUS WITH AS MANY AS 8 TO 15 INDIVIDUAL SELECTIONS REQUIRE ADVANCED PLANNING TO ENSURE EVERYTHING ARRIVES AT THE SERVING LINE ON TIME.

NEW ENGLAND FISH CHOWDER

Ingredients:

- 8 oz bacon, raw
- 1/4 cup 1 2/3 tablespoons bacon fat, rendered
- 2 lbs onions, fresh, chopped
- 1 lb celery, fresh, chopped
- 7 lbs potatoes, fresh, peeled, cubed
- 2 gal water
- 1 1/4 lbs butter
- 1 3/8 lbs flour, wheat, general purpose
- 1 1/3 lbs milk, nonfat, dry
- 2 gal 3 qts water, warm
- 10 lbs fish, flounder/sole fillet, raw, 2 inch pieces
- 1 Tbs. pepper, white, ground
- 1 Tbs. thyme, ground
- 1 Tbs. parsley, dehydrated, flaked
- 3 Tbs. salt

Instructions:

- Cook bacon until crisp. Drain; finely chop; set aside for use in Step 6. Reserve appropriate amount of bacon fat for use in Step 2.
- Saute onions and celery in bacon fat about 7 minutes or until crisp.
- Add potatoes and water to onion-celery mixture; cook until potatoes are almost tender but still firm, about 10 minutes.
- Blend butter or margarine and flour to form a roux; set aside for use in Step 6.
- Reconstitute milk; add to potato mixture. Cook until thickened or about 10 minutes.
- Add roux and cooked bacon to milk and potato mixture. Cook until thickened or about 10 minutes.
- Add fish, pepper, thyme, parsley and salt to mixture. Simmer 10 minutes. Internal temperature must reach 165 F. or higher for 15 seconds. Hold for service at 140 F. or higher.

NAVY BEAN SOUP

Ingredients:

- 6 1/4 lbs beans, white, dry
- 2 gal water, cold
- 5 gal ham broth (from mix)
- 1 lb carrots, fresh, shredded
- 2 lbs onions, fresh, chopped
- 1/3 tsp. pepper, black, ground
- 3 cups flour, wheat, general purpose
- 1 qt water, cold

Instructions:

- Pick over beans, removing discolored beans and foreign matter. Wash thoroughly in cold water.
- Cover with cold water; bring to a boil; boil 2 minutes. Turn off heat. Cover; let stand 1 hour.
- Prepare broth according to package directions.
- Add beans to stock; bring to a boil; cover; simmer 2 hours or until beans are tender.
- Add carrots, onions and pepper to bean mixture. Simmer 30 minutes.
- Blend flour and water to form a smooth paste. Stir into soup; cook 10 minutes. Internal temperature must reach 165 F. or higher for 15 seconds. Hold for service at 140 F. or higher.
- Precooked ham, cut into small pieces, may be added during the final step for added flavor.

POTATOES AU GRATIN

Ingredients:

- 25 1/2 lbs potatoes, fresh, peeled, sliced
- 2 gal 1 qt water
- 2 Tbs. salt
- 3 cups butter, melted
- 3 cups flour, wheat, general purpose
- 1 qt milk, nonfat, dry
- 1 gal 1 1/4 qts water, warm
- 2 Tbs. salt
- 1/3 tsp. pepper, white, ground
- 1 1/2 lbs cheese, cheddar, shredded
- 1 Tbs. mustard, dry
- 1 lb breadcrumbs, dry, ground, fine
- 1 cup butter, melted

Instructions:

- Cover potatoes with salted water; bring to a boil; cook 10 minutes or until tender.
- Drain well. Place about 8 pounds or 1 1/2 gallons potatoes in each steam table pan. Set aside for use in Step 6.
- Melt butter. Blend butter and flour together using wire whip: stir until smooth.
- Reconstitute milk; bring to just below boiling. DO NOT BOIL. Add milk to flour mixture stirring constantly. Add salt and pepper. Simmer 10 to 15 minutes or until thickened. Stir as necessary.
- Add cheese and mustard to sauce. Stir until cheese is melted.
- Pour 2 1/3 quarts sauce evenly over potatoes in each pan.
- Mix crumbs and butter or margarine. Sprinkle 1 1/3 cups crumbs over potatoes in each pan.
- Using a convection oven, bake in 325 F. for 30 minutes on low fan, open vent or until browned. Hold for service at 140 F. or higher.

BRUSSELS SPROUTS POLONAISE

Ingredients:

- 20 lbs Brussels sprouts, frozen
- 2 gal water, boiling
- 1 Tbs. salt
- 1 lb breadcrumbs, dry, ground, fine
- 1 cup butter, melted
- 9 eggs, hard cooked, chopped

Instructions:

- Add frozen brussels sprouts to boiling, salted water; return to boil; cook UNCOVERED for 7 to 9 minutes. Cover; reduce heat; cook 3 minutes or until tender. Drain. Place an equal quantity in each pan.
- Brown crumbs in butter or margarine. Sprinkle 1 cup crumbs over brussels sprouts in each pan.
- Garnish with hard cooked eggs. Heat to 145 F. or higher for 15 seconds. Hold at 140 F. or higher for service.

MONTEREY EGG BAKE

Ingredients:

- ¼ cup ⅓ tablespoon cooking spray, nonstick
- 9 ½ lbs potatoes, white, frozen, shredded, hashbrown
- 4 ⅛ lbs tomatoes, canned, diced, drained
- 2 ¼ lbs cheese, cheddar, lowfat, shredded
- 2 ¼ lbs cheese, Monterey jack, reduced fat, shredded
- 2 lbs peppers, green, fresh, chopped
- 2 lbs corn, frozen, whole kernel
- 2 ½ cups pepper, chili, green, canned, chopped, drained
- 1 ⅛ lbs onions, green, fresh, sliced
- 1 Tbs. salt
- 1 Tbs. pepper, white, ground
- 2 gal 2 qts egg substitute, pasteurized
- 1 qt 1 ¾ cup water
- 1 ¼ cup milk, nonfat, dry

Instructions:

- Lightly spray each steam table pan with non-stick cooking spray.
- Combine potatoes, tomatoes, cheddar cheese, Monterey jack cheese, green pepper, corn, green chilies, green onions, salt, and pepper; mix well.
- Place 2 ¼ quarts of potato mixture into each steam table pan.
- Combine egg substitute, water and nonfat dry milk; blend until mixed.
- Pour 1 ¾ quarts of egg mixture into each steam table pan; stir to combine.
- Using a convection oven, bake at 325 F. for 55 to 65 minutes. Internal temperature must reach 145 F. or higher for 15 seconds. Hold for service at 140 F. or higher.

RED CABBAGE WITH SWEET AND SOUR SAUCE

Ingredients:

- 2 ½ cups butter, melted
- 18 lbs cabbage, red, fresh, chopped
- 2 lbs apples, fresh, medium, unpeeled, diced
- 3 cups vinegar, distilled
- 2 ⅛ cups sugar, brown, packed
- ¼ cup ⅓ tablespoon salt
- ¼ cup ⅓ tablespoon cloves, ground
- 7 each bay leaf, whole, dried

Instructions:

- Place 1 ¼ cups butter or margarine in each roasting pan.
- Add 9 pounds or 11 ¼ quarts cabbage and 5 ½ cups apples to each pan. Mix thoroughly.
- Cook at low heat 30 minutes, stirring frequently to avoid scorching.
- Combine vinegar, brown sugar, salt, cloves and bay leaves.
- Pour vinegar mixture evenly over hot cabbage and apples in each pan.
- Simmer 2 to 3 minutes to blend seasonings. Remove bay leaves. Internal temperature must reach 145 F. or higher for 15 seconds. Hold at 140 F. or higher for service.

CREAMED CHIPPED BEEF (S.O.S.)

Ingredients:

- 7 lbs beef, chipped, dried, chopped
- 1 gal water, warm
- 1 3/4 lbs milk, nonfat, dry
- 3 gal 3 qts water, warm
- 1 1/2 lbs margarine, softened
- 2 1/4 lbs flour, wheat, general purpose
- 2 Tbs. pepper, black, ground

Instructions:

- Separate dried beef slices, cut into 1-inch slices.
- Place beef in 190 F. water. Soak 5 minutes. Drain thoroughly.
- Reconstitute milk. Heat to just below boiling. DO NOT BOIL.
- Combine butter or margarine with flour and pepper; add to milk, stirring constantly. Cook 5 minutes until thickened.
- Add beef to sauce; blend well. Internal temperature must reach 145 F. or higher for 15 seconds. Hold for service at 140 F. or higher.

NOODLES JEFFERSON

Ingredients:

- 6 gal water, warm
- 3 Tbs. salt
- 3 Tbs. oil, salad
- 9 lbs noodles, egg
- 2 1/2 cups butter, melted
- 1 Tbs. salt
- 1 Tbs. pepper, black, ground
- 2 lbs cheese, parmesan, grated

Instructions:

- Add salt and oil to water; heat to a rolling boil.
- Slowly add noodles, stirring constantly, until water boils again. Cook about 8 to 10 minutes or until tender. Drain thoroughly.
- Add butter, salt and pepper to noodles. Stir well.
- Add cheese; toss well, Hold for service at 140 F. or higher.

FRIJOLE SALAD

Ingredients:

- 3 qts beans, kidney, dark red, canned, drained
- 2 qts salad dressing, French
- 8 5/8 lbs cabbage, green, fresh, shredded
- 6 1/3 lbs tomatoes, fresh, chopped
- 3 2/3 lbs cucumbers, fresh, peeled, sliced

Instructions:

- Drain beans; rinse well; drain.
- Combine beans and French dressing.
- Cover; refrigerate at least 6 hours. Hold for service at 41 F. or lower.
- Add cabbage, tomatoes, and cucumbers just before serving. Mix lightly.

MEAT LOAF

Ingredients:

– 30 lbs beef, ground, bulk, raw, 90% lean
– 3 ¾ lbs breadcrumbs
– ¼ cup 2 ⅓ tsp. salt
– 1 Tbs. pepper, black, ground
– 1 Tbs. garlic powder
– 1 cup milk, nonfat, dry
– 1 qt 1 ½ cups water
– 1 lb celery, fresh, chopped
– 1 lb onions, fresh, chopped
– 1 lb peppers, green, fresh, chopped
– 1 qt ½ cup eggs, whole, frozen
– 1 qt 1 ¾ cups juice, tomato, canned

Instructions:

– Combine beef with breadcrumbs, salt, pepper and garlic; mix until well blended.
– Reconstitute milk.
– Add milk, celery, onions, sweet peppers, eggs, and tomato juice. Mix lightly but thoroughly. DO NOT OVER MIX.
– Place 11 pounds 6 ounces meat mixture into each steam table pan and divide into 2 loaves per pan.
– Using a convection oven, bake 1 hour 15 minutes at 300 F. Internal temperature must reach 155 F. or higher for 15 seconds. Skim off excess fat and liquid during cooking.
– Let stand 20 minutes before slicing. Cut 13 slices per loaf. Hold for service at 140 F. or higher.

SPICED SHRIMP

Ingredients:

- 12 lbs shrimp, frozen, raw, peeled, deveined
- 1 qt water, boiling
- 2 qts vinegar, distilled
- 1/4 cup 2 1/3 tablespoons pepper, red, ground
- 1/4 cup 2 1/3 tablespoons mustard, dry
- 1/4 cup 1/3 tablespoon celery seed
- 2 Tbs. paprika, ground
- 1 Tbs. ginger, ground
- 1 Tbs. mace, ground
- 1 Tbs. cinnamon, ground
- 1/3 tsp. cloves, ground
- 12 each, bay leaf, whole, dried
- 4 lbs lettuce, fresh, leaf, red
- 13 each lemons, fresh

Instructions:

- Place shrimp in boiling water, add vinegar and spices, cover; return to a boil. Uncover; reduce heat; simmer 2 to 3 minutes. Internal temperature must reach 145 F. or higher for 15 seconds. DO NOT OVER COOK. Drain immediately.
- Place shrimp in single layer on pans. Refrigerate at 41 F. or lower for use in Step 4.
- Line individual serving dishes with lettuce.
- Arrange 4 shrimp on lettuce in each dish. Hold for service at 41 F. or lower.
- Serve shrimp with 1 lemon wedge. Cut 8 wedges per lemon.

Note: In Step 3, prepared seafood cocktail sauce may be used.

BRAISED BEEF AND NOODLES

Ingredients:

- 30 lbs beef, diced, lean, raw
- 1 gal 3 qts water
- 4 lbs onions, fresh, sliced
- 1 qt catsup
- 3 Tbs. pepper, black, ground
- 3 Tbs. thyme, ground
- 1 Tbs. garlic powder
- 6 each bay leaf, whole, dried
- 1/4 cup 1 2/3 Tbs. salt
- 3 1/2 lbs noodles, egg
- 7 gal water, boiling
- 2 1/3 Tbs. salt
- 1 1/2 lbs flour, wheat, general purpose
- 1 qt 2 cups water, cold

Instructions:

- Place beef, water, onions, catsup, pepper, thyme, garlic powder, bay leaves and salt in steam-jacketed kettle or stock pot. Bring to a boil; reduce heat; cover; simmer about 2 hours or until tender. Skim off excess fat. Remove bay leaves.
- Add noodles to boiling salted water; return to a boil; cook 8 to 10 minutes or until tender; drain thoroughly.
- Combine flour and water to make smooth mixture; stir into beef mixture. Blend well. Return to boil. Reduce heat; cook 10 minutes or until thickened. Internal temperature must reach 145 F. or higher for 15 seconds.
- Add cooked noodles to beef mixture. Stir well. Hold for service at 140 F. or higher.

TAMALE PIE (GROUND BEEF)

Ingredients:

- 6 1/2 lbs corn meal
- 3 gal water, boiling
- 16 lbs beef, ground, bulk, raw, 90% lean
- 2 lbs onions, fresh, chopped
- 1 lb peppers, green, fresh, chopped
- 1 gal 2 qts tomatoes, canned, crushed, incl. liquids
- 1 gal 2/3 qts corn, canned, whole kernel, drained
- 3 qts olives, ripe, pitted, sliced, incl. liquids
- 1 cup chili powder, dark, ground
- 1/4 cup 2 1/3 Tbs. cumin, ground
- 3 1/3 Tbs. garlic powder
- 1 Tbs. salt
- 1 Tbs. pepper, red, ground
- 1/4 cup 1/3 tablespoon cooking spray, nonstick
- 3 lbs cheese, cheddar, grated

Instructions:

- Mix cornmeal; chili powder and salt together; gradually stir into boiling water. Bring to a boil.
- Reduce heat; simmer 25 minutes, stirring frequently until a stiff paste is formed. Set aside for use in Step 5.
- Cook beef with onions and peppers until beef loses its pink color, stirring to break apart. Drain or skim off excess fat.
- Add tomatoes, corn, olives, chili powder, cumin, salt, garlic powder, and red pepper to beef mixture; simmer 15 minutes, stirring frequently.
- Lightly spray each pan with non-stick spray. Spread 2 1/3 cup cornmeal paste over bottom and sides of each pan to form a thin crust.
- Pour 2 quarts meat mixture over crust in each pan.
- Spread 4 2/3 cups cornmeal paste evenly over meat mixture in each pan.
- Using a convection oven, bake at 325 F. 50 to 60 minutes on low fan, open vent; remove from oven. Internal temperature must reach 155 F. or higher for 15 seconds.
- Sprinkle 1 1/2 cups cheese evenly over each pan.
- Let stand 10 to 15 minutes to allow filling to firm and cheese to melt. Hold for service at 140 F. or higher. Cut 3 by 4.

CHUCK WAGON STEW (BEANS WITH BEEF)

Ingredients:

- 15 lbs beef, ground, bulk, raw, 90% lean
- 6 lbs onions, fresh, chopped
- 3 lbs peppers, green, fresh, chopped
- 3 1/2 cups catsup
- 6 gal beans, baked, w/pork, canned

Instructions:

- Cook beef with onions and peppers until it loses its pink color, stirring to break apart, in steam-jacketed kettle or stock pot. Drain or skim off excess fat.
- Add catsup and beans to beef, onion and pepper mixture. Stir well.
- Simmer for 20 minutes. Internal temperature must reach 155 F. or higher for 15 seconds. Hold for service at 140 F. or higher.

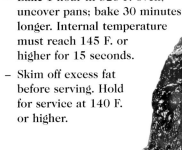

BAKED STUFFED PORK CHOPS

Ingredients:

- 31 1/4 lbs pork chop, boneless, 5 oz
- 1/4 cup 1/3 tablespoon cooking spray, nonstick
- 3 2/3 lbs bread, white, sliced
- 1 lb onions, fresh, chopped
- 1 Tbs. salt
- 1/3 Tbs. pepper, black, ground
- 2 Tbs. seasoning, poultry
- 1 cup eggs, whole, frozen
- 2 qts 2 cups water
- 4 lbs peppers, green, fresh, rings
- 1 qt 1 cup water

Instructions:

- Lightly spray griddle with non-stick cooking spray. Brown chops on griddle for 5 minutes on each side.
- Place 20 chops in each steam table pan.
- Combine bread, onions, salt, pepper, poultry seasoning, eggs, and water; mix lightly but thoroughly.
- Place 1 pepper ring on each chop; top with 1/4 cup bread mixture.
- Pour 1 cup water in each pan.
- Using a convection oven, bake 40-45 minutes on high fan, closed vent or until tender in 325 F. oven. Internal temperature must reach 145 F. or higher for 15 seconds. Hold for service at 140 F. or higher.

BARBECUED SPARERIBS

Ingredients:

- 75 lbs pork, spareribs, frozen, raw
- 4 gal water
- 3 3/4 cups sauce, chili
- 1 gal, 1 1/4 qts catsup
- 1 3/4 cups Worcestershire sauce
- 3/4 cup mustard, prepared
- 2 1/2 cups vinegar, distilled
- 3 Tbs. salt
- 3 Tbs. pepper, black, ground
- 1 Tbs. pepper, red, ground

Instructions:

- Cut ribs into serving size portions 10 to 12 ounces raw weight total or 2 to 4 ribs. Place ribs in steam-jacketed kettle or stock pot.
- Cover with water; bring to a boil; reduce heat; simmer 45 minutes or until tender. Drain ribs.
- Combine chili sauce, catsup, Worcestershire sauce, mustard, vinegar, salt, black and red pepper; bring to a boil. Reduce heat; simmer 5 minutes.
- Dip ribs in sauce to coat well. Overlap ribs in rows fat side up, in pans.
- Pour remaining sauce evenly over ribs in each steam table pan; cover pans.
- Bake 1 hour in 325 F. oven, uncover pans; bake 30 minutes longer. Internal temperature must reach 145 F. or higher for 15 seconds.
- Skim off excess fat before serving. Hold for service at 140 F. or higher.

HONEY GLAZED ROCK CORNISH HENS

Ingredients:

- 78 1/8 lbs Cornish hen, rock, raw, whole
- 1/4 cup 1/3 tablespoon cooking spray, nonstick
- 1 1/2 lbs sugar, brown, packed
- 2 cups honey
- 2 cups juice, orange

Instructions:

- Remove necks and giblets. Wash hens, inside and out, thoroughly under cold running water. Drain well; pat dry.
- Using sharp boning knife or cleaver, split hens in half lengthwise.
- Lightly spray sheet pans with non-stick cooking spray. Place each half skin side up, on sheet pans.
- Using a convection oven, bake at 325 F. for 30 minutes on high fan, closed vent.
- Heat brown sugar, honey and orange juice until sugar is melted to make a glaze.
- Remove hens from oven; brush tops with glaze.
- Return to convection oven; bake 20 minutes or until golden brown or done. Internal temperature must reach 165 F. or higher for 15 seconds.
- Brush remaining glaze over hens in each pan before serving. Hold for service at 140 F. or higher.

STEAK, CHEESE AND ONION SUBMARINE

Ingredients:

- 20 lbs onions, fresh, sliced
- 1/4 cup 1/3 Tbs. cooking spray, nonstick
- 25 lbs beef, steak, sandwich, thin slices, raw
- 100 sl cheese, American, sliced
- 100 each roll, French

Instructions:

- Lightly spray grill with non-stick cooking spray. Grill thinly sliced onions 5 to 6 minutes.
- Grill steaks on one side 30 seconds on lightly sprayed grill at 350 F. Turn steaks; cover half of steaks with cheese slices. Grill steaks 30 seconds. Internal temperature must reach 145 F. or higher for 15 seconds.
- Slice rolls in half lengthwise. Place 1 steak on bottom half of each roll. Add steak with cheese on top. Add 1/3 cup grilled onions on each sandwich.
- Cover with top half of roll. Hold at 140 F. or higher for service.

ROAST BEEF (PORTION 100 SLICES - 4 OUNCES)

Ingredients:

- 40 lbs. Beef, oven roast, thawed
- 2 tablespoons Pepper, black

Instructions:

- Sprinkle roasts with pepper
- Place fat side up in 18 by 24-inch pans, without crowding
- Insert meat thermometer into center of thickest part of main muscle DO NOT ADD WATER. DO NOT COVER.
- Roast 2 to 3 hours in 325 degrees F oven, depending on size of roasts, to desired degree of doneness. (Allow about 20 minutes per pound for medium; about 18 minutes per pound for rare.) If roasts are frozen, cooking time will be increased by 1 hour or more.
- Remove roasts from oven when meat thermometer registers 140 degrees F.-rare; 160 degrees F.-medium; and 170 degrees F.-well done. Internal temperature will rise about 10 degrees F. during 20 minute standing period.
- Let stand 20 minutes before slicing.

CHIPPER FISH

Ingredients:

- 30 lbs fish, flounder/sole fillet, raw
- 2 qts salad dressing, French
- 2 lbs potato chips
- 2 3/4 lbs cheese, cheddar, shredded

Instructions:

- Separate fillets; cut into 4 1/2 ounce portions, if necessary. Dip fillets in French dressing; place in single layers on sheet pans.
- Crush chips. Combine chips and cheese. Sprinkle about 1 quart mixture over fish in each pan.
- Using a convection oven, bake 7 minutes at 350 F. on high fan, closed vent, or until done. Internal temperature must reach 145 F. or higher for 15 seconds. Hold for service at 140 F. or higher.

VEGETABLE LASAGNA

Ingredients:

- 5 3/4 lbs noodles, lasagna, uncooked
- 1/2 cup oil, canola
- 1 1/4 lbs squash, fresh, zucchini, sliced
- 2 cups mushrooms, canned, sliced, white
- 1 lb onions, fresh, chopped
- 1 cup flour, wheat, general purpose
- 6 7/8 lbs broccoli, frozen, cut
- 1 gal 3 1/2 qts sauce, tomato, canned
- 1 qt 3 cups tomato paste, canned
- 3/4 cup oregano, crushed
- 1 Tbs. garlic powder
- 2 gals cheese, cottage, lowfat
- 1/2 cup parsley, dehydrated, flaked
- 1 Tbs. garlic powder
- 1 lb breadcrumbs
- 1 cup cheese, parmesan, grated
- 3 3/4 lbs cheese, mozzarella, part skim, shredded

Instructions:

- Cook lasagna noodles in a steam-jacketed kettle for 10 to 12 minutes, until tender. Drain. Hold in cold water.
- In a small kettle, heat vegetable oil. Add the zucchini, drained mushrooms, and onions. Saute for 3 minutes or until zucchini is slightly tender. Stir in flour, cook 3 minutes. Remove from heat and set aside.
- Place broccoli in a steam table pan and steam for 6 minutes, or until tender. Drain well and set aside.
- In a steam kettle, heat the tomato sauce and tomato paste. Add oregano and garlic powder. Simmer, uncovered for 30 minutes.
- Add the sauteed vegetables and steamed broccoli to the tomato sauce. Stir to combine. Simmer for 10 minutes.
- In a large bowl, combine the cottage cheese, parsley, garlic powder, and bread crumbs. Mix well.
- Combine parmesan cheese and mozzarella cheese.
- Spread 1 cup vegetable sauce on the bottom of each steam table pan to prevent sticking.
- Assembly: First layer: 7 1/2 lasagna noodles; 1 quart of cottage cheese mixture; 1 quart and 1 cup of vegetable sauce; 2 1/4 cups parmesan-mozzarella cheese mixture; Second layer: repeat first layer; Third layer: 7 1/2 lasagna noodles; 2 1/2 cups vegetable sauce.
- Sprinkle 1/2 cup parmesan cheese over each pan of lasagna. Cover with wrap or foil. Using a convection oven, bake at 350 F. for 40 minutes until bubbling. Internal temperature must reach 145 F. or higher for 15 seconds.
- Remove from oven and allow to set for 15 minutes before serving. Cut each pan 5 by 5 (25 portions per pan). Hold for service at 140 F. or higher.

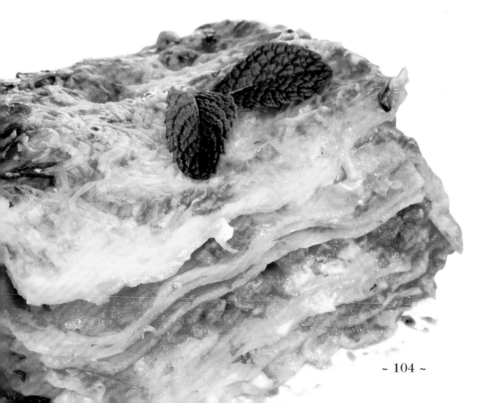

VEGETARIAN HEARTY BURGER

Ingredients:

– 3 qts 2 cups egg whites

– 4 1/2 lbs cheese, mozzarella, part skim, shredded

– 2 7/8 lbs onions, fresh, grated

– 1 1/2 cups soy sauce

– 8 5/8 lbs cereal, oatmeal, rolled

– 1 5/8 lbs walnuts, shelled, chopped

– 1/2 cup garlic powder

– 1/4 cup 1/3 Tbs. sage, ground

– 1/4 cup 1/3 Tbs.cooking spray, nonstick

– 100 each roll, sandwich buns, split

Instructions:

– Place egg whites, cheese, onions, and soy sauce in mixer bowl. Using a dough hook, mix on low speed 1 minute or until well blended.

– Add oats, walnuts, garlic powder, and sage; mix on low speed 1 minute. Scrape down sides; continue mixing 30 seconds, or until well blended. Refrigerate mixture at least one hour to allow mixture to absorb moisture. Refrigerate at 41 F. or lower.

– Shape 3 1/2 ounce balls. Place 20 balls on each sheet pan. Cover with parchment paper; flatten into burgers by pressing down with another sheet pan to a thickness of 1/2 inch. Mixture will be very moist and fragile.

– Grill burgers on lightly sprayed griddle at 400 F. for 6 minutes or bake on lightly sprayed sheet pans in a convection oven at 350 F. for 15 to 20 minutes on high fan, open vent or until golden brown. Internal temperature must reach 145 F. or higher for 15 seconds.

– Serve on buns. Hold for service at 140 F. or higher.

DEVIL'S FOOD CAKE

Ingredients:

– 2 3/4 lbs flour, wheat, general purpose

– 4 3/8 lbs sugar, granulated

– 2 1/3 Tbs. salt

– 3 1/3 Tbs. baking soda

– 1 1/4 lbs cocoa

– 1 3/4 cups milk, nonfat, dry

– 1 3/4 lbs shortening

– 1 qt 1 cup water

– 2 1/2 lbs eggs, whole, frozen

– 2 1/2 cups water

– 2 Tbs. extract, vanilla

– 1/4 cup 1/3 Tbs. cooking spray, nonstick

Instructions:

– Sift together flour, sugar, salt, baking soda, cocoa and milk into mixer bowl.

– Blend shortening with dry ingredients. Add water gradually; beat at low speed 2 minutes or until blended. Beat at medium speed 2 minutes. Scrape down bowl.

– Combine eggs, water, and vanilla; add slowly to mixture while beating at low speed 1 minute. Scrape down bowl. Beat at medium speed 3 minutes.

– Lightly spray each pan with non-stick cooking spray. Pour 4 1/2 quarts batter into each greased and floured pan. Spread evenly.

– Using a convection oven, bake at 300 F. for 25 to 35 minutes or until done on low fan, open vent.

– Cool; frost if desired. Cut 6 by 9.

BLUEBERRY CRUNCH (BLUEBERRY PIE FILLING)

Ingredients:

- 21 1/4 lbs pie filling, blueberry, prepared
- 1/4 cup 1/3 tbsp cooking spray, nonstick
- 1/4 cup 2 1/3 tbsp juice, lemon
- 5 lbs cake mix, yellow
- 1 lb coconut, prepared, sweetened flakes
- 1 lb margarine, softened

Instructions:

- Spray each pan with non-stick cooking spray. Spread 4 1/2 quarts of pie filling into each sprayed sheet pan. Sprinkle 3 tablespoons of lemon juice on top of mixture in each pan.
- Combine cake mix and coconut; add margarine; mix until crumbly.
- Sprinkle 2 3/4 quarts of mixture over each pan.
- Using a convection oven, bake at 325 F. for 30 minutes or until lightly browned on low fan, open vent.
- Cut 6 by 9.

Note: In Step 2, 1 pound chopped unsalted nuts may be substituted for coconut, per 100 servings.

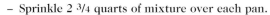

ABRACADABRA BARS

Ingredients:

- 4 1/2 lbs flour, wheat, general purpose
- 2 2/3 tbsp baking soda
- 1 Tbs. salt
- 1 Tbs. cinnamon, ground
- 3/8 tsp nutmeg, ground
- 3/8 tsp cloves, ground
- 3/8 tsp ginger, ground
- 4 7/8 lbs sweet potatoes, canned, w/syrup
- 3 1/3 lbs sugar, granulated
- 1 3/4 cups shortening
- 1/4 cup 1 2/3 tbsp extract, vanilla
- 1 7/8 lbs raisins
- 1/4 cup 1/3 tbsp cooking spray, nonstick

Instructions:

- Combine flour, baking soda, salt, cinnamon, nutmeg, cloves, and ginger.
- Drain sweet potatoes, mash and set aside. Cream sugar and shortening. Add sweet potatoes and vanilla to the creamed sugar and shortening, beat on medium speed 1 minute; scrape down bowl. Beat with paddle on high speed 1 minute or until light and fluffy. Scrape down bowl.
- Gradually add dry ingredients to sweet potato mixture, while mixing on low speed 1 minute. Scrape down bowl; mix on medium speed 30 seconds or until just blended.
- Fold in raisins at low speed 30 seconds.
- Spray sheet pans very lightly with non-stick cooking spray. Using a rolling pin, spread 7 pounds 5 ounces mixture evenly in each pan.
- Using a convection oven, bake at 325 F. 16 to 18 minutes until bars are lightly browned on low fan, open vent. Cool. Cut into bars 6 by 18.

CRUMB CAKE SNICKERDOODLE

Ingredients:

- 2 1/2 cups shortening
- 3 lbs sugar, granulated
- 1 3/4 lbs eggs, whole, frozen
- 5 lbs flour, wheat, general purpose
- 1/4 cup 2 tbsp baking powder
- 3/4 cup milk, nonfat, dry
- 1 Tbs. nutmeg, ground
- 1 Tbs. salt
- 3 3/4 cups water
- 1 Tbs. extract, vanilla
- 1 3/4 lbs raisins
- 1 1/4 lbs nuts, unsalted, chopped, coarsely
- 1/4 cup 1/3 tbsp cooking spray, nonstick
- 1 1/3 lbs sugar, brown, packed
- 1 cup margarine
- 1/4 cup 1/3 tbsp cinnamon, ground
- 3 cups yellow cake (crumbs)

Instructions:

- Place shortening and sugar in mixer bowl; cream at medium speed until light and fluffy.
- Add eggs; beat at medium speed 2 minutes or until light and fluffy.
- Sift together flour, baking powder, milk, nutmeg, and salt.
- Add vanilla to water; add alternately with dry ingredients to mixture. Mix 1 1/2 minutes at low speed.
- Fold raisins and nuts into batter.
- Lightly spray each pan with non-stick cooking spray. Pour about 3 1/2 quarts of batter into each lightly sprayed pan.
- Mix brown sugar, butter or margarine, cinnamon, and cake crumbs until mixture resembles cornmeal. Sprinkle about 1 quart of mixture over batter in each pan.
- Using a convection oven, bake at 300 F. for 20 to 25 minutes or until done on low fan, open vent.
- Cool; cut 6 by 9.

PEANUT BUTTER COOKIES

Sugar Cookie mix

Ingredients:

- 10 lbs cookie mix, sugar
- 3 cups water
- 1 qt 1/2 cup peanut butter

Instructions:

- Prepare sugar cookie mix according to package directions. Add water and peanut butter. Mix at low speed 1 minute. DO NOT OVER MIX.
- Drop by slightly rounded tablespoons. Place in rows, 4 by 6, on ungreased pans; using a fork, flatten to 1/4 inch thickness, forming a crisscross pattern.
- Using a convection oven, bake at 325 F. for 10 to 12 minutes or until lightly browned on high fan, open vent.
- Loosen cookies from pans while still warm.

Chapter 6
SPECIAL MENUS AND RECIPES

FOLLOWING IS A HISTORICAL SAMPLING of special menus served aboard ships of the United States Navy. Note how the recipes collected for this book are a reflection of the entrées in these menus.

A Special Yuletide Menu
U.S.S. Massachusetts (1862)

Roasted beef, pig, raccoon, rabbit, turkey, and ham
Boiled duck,
Baked, roasted and stewed chicken
Raw, fried, and stewed oysters
Baked, boiled, and fried fish
Sweet potatoes
Baked potatoes
Tomatoes
Corn
Plum, apple, and orange pudding
Apple mincemeat, and pumpkin pies
Plain, fruit and sponge cakes
Coffee and water

Thanksgiving Menu
U.S.S. Raleigh, Hong Kong, 1905

Creamed Asparagus Bouillon

Hors d'oeuvres

Roast Turkey

Oyster Dressing

Cranberry Sauce

Celery

Creamed Potatoes

Young Onions a la Hollandaise

Steamed Cabbage and White Sauce

Lemon, Pumpkin, and Mince Pies

Fruit Cake

Candy, Assorted Nuts

Cigars - Cigarettes

Iced tea

A Christmas Dinne
U.S.S. Nevada (1929)

Sweet Pickles · Green Olives

Oyster Soup

Crackers

Roast Young Turkey

Oyster Dressing · Giblet Gravy

Cranberry Sauce

Candied Sweet Potatoes

Asparagus Tips, Drawn Butter

Pumpkin Pie

Neapolitan Ice Cream · Ice Cream

Coffee

Oranges · Apples · Nuts

Hard candies · Cigarettes

A Thanksgiving Dinner
the U.S.S. Midway (1945)

MENU

Cream of Tomato Soup • Saltine Crackers

Ripe Olives • Mixed Pickles

Stuffed Celery Hearts

Roast Young Tom Turkey

Giblet Gravy • Sage Dressing

Cherry Jam

Baked Spiced Ham

Buttered Peas • Buttered Carrots

Candied Sweet Potatoes • Mashed Potato

Hot Parker House Rolls and Butter

Ice cream • Hot Mince Pie

Iced Fresh Lemonade

Cigars • Cigarettes

A Thanksgiving Dinner
the U.S.S. Midway (1990)

Chilled Fruit Ambrosia

Shrimp Cocktail

Midway Salad Bar

Roast Tom Turkey • Virginia Baked Ham

W/Cornbread Dressing • w/Pineapple Raisin Sauce

Giblet Gravy

Chilled Cranberry Sauce

Candied Sweet Potatoes • Mashed Potatoes

Peas w/Sliced Mushrooms • Buttered Green Beans

Assorted Breads

Hot Dinner Rolls • Hot Cornbread

Holiday Fruit Cake

Pumpkin Pie w/Whipped Topping

Assorted Ice Cream

Fruit Combo

Mixed Nuts • Hard Candies

Iced Tea • Coffee • Fruit Punch

A *U.S.S. Midway* menu for the General Mess (1992)

Following is a menu published for the *U.S.S. Midway* mess for one day. (You may want to compare it with what was served aboard such ships as the *U.S.S. Ganges* or the *U.S.S. Weehawken*. The "Speed Line" entry was for the forward galley that served a simple menu from 1130, until 1830. The forward galley reopened at 0700, when it served freshly cooked donuts to coffee mess representatives from throughout the ship.

BREAKFAST: *Chilled fresh fruits, chilled fruit juices, hot oatmeal, hard boiled eggs, grilled eggs to order, assorted omelets to order, oven fried bacon, minced beef on biscuits, hash brown potatoes, pancakes w/syrup.*

LUNCH: *Manhattan clam chowder, savory baked chicken, Swedish meat balls, egg noodles, deviled oven fries, chicken gravy, carrots amandine, herbed green beans, hot cloverleaf rolls, dessert bar, and salad bar.*

DINNER: *Minestrone soup, chicken and Italian vegetable pasta, glazed ham, pineapple sauce, cottage fried potatoes, peas and mushrooms, seasoned cauliflower, hot dinner rolls, dessert bar, and salad bar.*

MID-RATS: *(Served from 2330, until 0200). Eggs to order, omelets to order, glazed ham, savory baked chicken, hash brown potatoes, biscuits and gravy, chilled fresh fruit.*

SPEED LINE: *Grilled cheeseburgers, simmered frankfurters, chili w/o beans, French fries, baked beans.*

THE GOLDEN TROUGH

During the Vietnam War, the stewards who served the Admiral Commanding Attack Carrier Striking Force SEVENTH Fleet, published a recipe book titled *The Golden Trough*. This limited compilation of recipes reflects the dishes served in the Flag Mess aboard the aircraft carriers hosting the admiral and his staff. I am including a number of those recipes here so my reader might compare them with those served in the officers' mess in Chapter One.

BEEF AND VERMICELLI SOUP

Ingredients:

- ¹/₄ lb. thin Chinese noodles or vermicelli
- Boiling water to cover noodles
- 2 Tbs. cornstarch
- ¹/₄ cup water
- ¹/₂ lb. ground meat
- 1 tsp. salt
- ¹/₄ tsp. pepper
- 4 Tbs. oil
- 6 cups beef broth
- 2 tbs. soy sauce
- 3 scallions, cut in ¹/₂ inch pieces

Instructions:

- Break the noodles in 2 inch lengths. Cover with boiling water and let soak for 5 minutes; drain well. Mix together the cornstarch and water. Mix the meat, salt, pepper, and cornstarch mixture. Fry the mixture in hot oil until brown. Bring the broth to a boil; add the noodles and cook for 5 minutes. Carefully drop the meat mixture into the broth and cook for 5 minutes. Stir in the soy sauce and scallions. Cook 3 minutes. Serves 6-8.

SOUPE A L'OIGNON (FRENCH ONION SOUP)

Ingredients:

- 4 Tbs. butter
- 2 Tbs. vegetable oil
- 2 lbs. onions, thinly cut (about 7 cups)
- 1 tsp. salt
- 3 Tbs. flour
- 2 qts. beef stock, fresh or canned, or beef and chicken stock combined.

Instructions:

- Melt the butter with the oil over moderate heat in a heavy 4 or 5 quart sauce pan or soup kettle. Stir in the onions and 1 teaspoon salt. Cook uncovered over low heat, stirring occasionally, for 20 to 30 minutes, or until the onions are rich golden brown. Remove the pan from the heat. In a separate saucepan, bring the stock to a simmer, then stir the hot stock into the onions. Return the soup to low heat and simmer partially covered for another 30 or 40 minutes, skimming off any fat. Salt and pepper to taste.

CHEESE-PUFFED PORK CHOPS

Ingredients:

- 4 salt chops
  1 inch thick
- Salt and pepper
- 2 tsp. butter
- 1/3 cup flour
- 2/3 cup milk
- 1 egg slightly beaten
- 1 small onion, grated
- 1/2 cup grated cheese

Instructions:

- Brown pork chops - sprinkle with salt and pepper. Melt butter in a sauce pan and blend in flour; slowly stir in milk. Cook, stirring constantly until the mixture makes a very thick paste. Add the egg and beat well, cooking until the mixture is shimmy. Stir in the onions, cheese, salt and pepper. Mix well. Turn over chops and put a spoonful of batter on top of each chop. Brown bottom of the chops for 5 minutes. Bake in 350-degree oven for 30 minutes.
  Serves 2-3.

JAMES BEARD MEAT LOAF

Ingredients:

- 2 lbs. of ground beef
- 1 lb. of ground pork
- 2 garlic cloves,
  finely chopped
- 1 fairly large onion,
  finely chopped
- 1 tsp. salt
- 1 tsp. freshly ground
  black pepper
- 1 crumbled bay leaf
- 1/2 tsp. crumbled
  thyme leaves
- 1 tsp. freshly chopped
  green bell pepper
- 1/2 cup dry
  bread crumbs
- 2 eggs
- Bacon or salt pork

Instructions:

- Mix all ingredients, except bacon, thoroughly and knead with the fingers until the mixture is thoroughly blended. Form into a long loaf or cake and press firmly. Arrange enough slices of bacon or salt pork on the bottom of a baking pan to hold the meat loaf. Place meat loaf on top of the bacon slices and brush the loaf with butter. Cross the top of the loaf with 2 to 4 additional slices of bacon. Bake at 325 degrees F., basting occasionally, for 1 1/2 to 1 3/4 hours, or until the MEAT LOAF is cooked through.

- Basting the MEAT LOAF during cooking will make your final product more moist. If you are going to serve the meat loaf hot, let it stand on a hot platter for 10 to 15 minutes to let the juices settle. Served cold, it makes superb sandwiches.

BROCCOLI SOUFFLÉ

Ingredients:

– 1 Tbs. minced shallot
   or green onions

– 1/4 tsp. salt

– 5 egg yolks, beaten

– A pinch of salt

– 3 Tbs. flour

– 1 cup milk

– 4 Tbs. butter

– 3/4 cup blanched,
   chopped broccoli

– 5 egg whites

– 1/3 to 1/2 cup
   (1 1/2 to 2 oz.)
   grated Swiss cheese

Instructions:

– Butter a 6-cup soufflé mold and
sprinkle with a small amount of the
cheese. Preheat oven to 400 degrees. In
a medium-sized sauce pan, combine flour,
milk, and 3 tbs. butter into a sauce base. Cook the shallot
or onions in the remaining 1 tbs. butter. Add the broccoli
and salt, and stir over moderately high heat for several
minutes to evaporate as much moisture as possible from
the broccoli. Remove from heat. Beat the egg yolks into
the sauce base. Stir in the broccoli. Correct the seasoning.
Beat the egg whites and salt until stiff. Stir in one fourth
of them into the sauce. Stir all but a tablespoon of the
cheese. Fold in the rest of the egg whites and turn the
mixture into the prepared mold. Sprinkle the remaining
cheese on top and set on a rack in the middle level of a
pre-heated oven. Turn heat down to 375 degrees and
bake for 25 to 30 minutes. Serves 6

BEAN SALAD ESCALON

*Good with menu including prime rib roast with horseradish, rice pilaf, platter of
fresh raw vegetables, garlic bread and apple pie for dessert.*

Ingredients:

– 1 (1-lb) can cut
   green beans

– 1 (1-lb) can red
   kidney beans

– 1 (1-lb) can
   garbanzo beans

– 1 (8-oz) can pitted
   ripe olives (optional)

– 1 red onion,
   thinly sliced

– 1/2 cup minced
   green bell pepper

– 1/2 cup oil

– 1/3 cup California
   red wine vinegar

– 1/4 cup California
   burgundy, claret, or
   other red dinner wine

– 1/2 cup granulated sugar

– 1/4 tsp. basil,
   or 1/4 tsp. mixed
   salad herbs

– 1/4 tsp. garlic powder

Instructions:

– Drain beans and olives; combine with onion and green
pepper. Combine the remaining ingredients; pour over bean
mixture. Cover; refrigerate several hours or overnight.

CLAFOUTI LIMOUSIN

Ingredients:

Cherry Filling

– 4 cups (1 1/2 pounds) pitted sweet black or red cherries

– 1 Tbs. lemon juice

– 3/4 cup sugar

– 1/8 teaspoon salt

– 2 Tbs. flour

– 2 Tbs. butter

Pudding Batter

– 1 3/4 cups sifted all-purpose flour

– 2 1/2 tsp. double-acting baking powder

– 1/2 tsp. salt

– 1 1/2 tsp. vanilla extract

– 1/2 cup softened butter

– 3/4 cup sugar

– 1 large egg

– 2/3 cup milk

Instructions:

– Combine the cherries with the lemon juice and put them in an 8 by 8 by 2 inch greased baking dish. Mix the sugar, salt and flour and sprinkle over the cherries. Dot with butter. Set aside while making the pudding batter. Sift together the first three ingredients. Set aside. Mix the vanilla extract with the butter and gradually blend in the sugar. Beat in the egg. Add the flour mixture alternately with the milk. Beat the batter for 30 seconds, then spread it over the cherries. Bake in a preheated moderate oven (350 degrees) 50 minutes, or until a toothpick inserted into the center comes out clean. Serve warm or cold. Serves 6-8.

CHOCOLATE RUM ICE CREAM

Ingredients:

– 2 cups milk

– 3/4 cup sugar

– 4 tsp. flour

– 1/2 tsp. salt

– 2 oz. Unsweetened chocolate, grated or shredded

– 3 egg yolks or 2 whole eggs

– 2 tsp. vanilla extract

– 2 cups light cream

– 1 Tbs. rum

Instructions:

– Scald the milk in the top of a double boiler. Add 2 oz. of chocolate and stir until melted. Mix the sugar, flour and salt together. Add the hot milk chocolate mixture to the dry ingredients and return the mixture to the double boiler. Stir over boiling water until thickened. Beat the egg yolks (or whole eggs) and add a small portion of the hot mixture. Add the egg mixture to the hot milk chocolate mixture in the double boiler and cook, stirring occasionally, until the mixture coats a metal spoon. Add the vanilla, cream and rum. Freeze in a hand-crank freezer. Makes about 1 1/2 quarts.

Books:

Alden, John D., Commander, U.S. Navy, Ret. <u>The American Steel Navy.</u> U.S. Naval Institute Press, Annapolis, Maryland. 1972.

Brady, W.N. <u>The Kedge Anchor; Or Young Sailor's Assistant: Appertaining to the Practical Evolutions of Modern Seamanship.</u> Unknown binding, 1872.

Chapelle, Howard I. <u>The History of the American Sailing Navy.</u> W.W. Norton & Co., Inc. 1949.

Davis, William C. <u>A Taste of War.</u> Stackpole Books, Mechanicsburg, PA 2003.

Grossman, Anne C. and Thomas, Lisa G. <u>Lobscouse & Spotted Dog.</u> W.W. Norton & Co., New York. 1997.

Heck, J. G. <u>Iconographic Encyclopedia of Sciences, Literature and Art,</u> vol.3. Unknown binding. 1851.

Johnston, Stanley. <u>Queen of the Flat-Tops, The U.S.S. Lexington and the Coral Sea Battle.</u> E.P. Dutton & Co., Inc., New York. 1942.

Krey, Otto. <u>Ship's Cook and Baker.</u> Cornell Maritime Press, New York. 1942.

Krey, Otto. <u>Ship Steward's</u> Handbook. Cornell Maritime Press, New York. 1942.

McGowan, David. <u>Sailor, A Pictorial History.</u> David Mckay Company, Inc. New York. 1977.

Miller, Nathan. <u>The U.S. Navy, An Illustrated History.</u> U.S. Naval Institute Press, Annapolis, Maryland, 1977.

O'Brian, Patrick. <u>Men-Of -War.</u> W.W. Norton & Co., New York. 1974.

Ringle, Dennis J. <u>Life in Mr. Lincoln's Navy.</u> U.S. Naval Institute Press, Annapolis, Maryland, 1998.

Schofield, William G., Captain, USNR. <u>Destroyers - 60 Years.</u> Burdette & Co., Boston Massachusetts, 1962.

Articles:

Anderson, Richard M. "The Navy Ration." <u>U.S. Naval Institute Proceedings.</u> 92 (1966): 186-88.

Crumpacker, J. W., Commander. "Supplying the Fleet for 150 Years." <u>U.S. Naval Institute Proceedings.</u> 71 (1945): 705-13.

Decker, Benton C., Lieutenant. "The Consolidated Mess of the Crew of the U.S.S. Indiana." <u>U.S. Naval Institute Proceedings.</u> 23 (1887): 463-72.

Dyer, George P., Paymaster. "The Modern General Mess." <u>U.S. Naval Institute Proceedings.</u> 32 (1906): 621-43.

Dyer, George P., Paymaster. "The Ship's General Mess." <u>U.S. Naval Institute Proceedings.</u> 39 (1913): 1589-1606.

Foster, E. D. Lieutenant, "Cafeteria Afloat." <u>U.S. Naval Institute Proceedings.</u> 63 (1937): 19-24.

Harrod, Fredrick S. "Jim Crow in the Navy (1798-1941)." <u>U.S. Naval Institute Proceedings.</u> 105 (1979): 47-53.

Harter, C. J. Commander. "Higher Education for Officers' Stewards & Cooks." U.S. Naval Institute Proceedings. 63 (1937): 321-28.

Peel, M. A., Jr., Lieutenant (SC). "Fleet Issue of Provisions." U.S. Naval Institute Proceedings. 69 (1943): 358-60.

Sharpe, Norville E. Captain. "Salt Horse to Sirloin." U.S. Naval Institute Proceedings. 80 (1954): 514-21.

Skillman, J. H. Commander (SC). "Eating Through the Years." U.S. Naval Institute Proceedings. 67 (1941): 361-67.

Skillman, J. H. Commander (SC). "Menu Planning." U.S. Naval Institute Proceedings. 67 (1941): 83-88.

U. S. Government Publications:

Arms, F. T. Paymaster. General Mess Manual and Cookbook for Use on Board Vessels Of the United States Navy. U.S. Navy Bureau of Supplies and Accounts. 1902.

Butowski, Dr. Harry A. Warships Associated with World War 2 in the Pacific - National Historic Landmark Theme Study, National Park Service History Division, May 1985.

Roach, John C. Old Ironsides, U.S. Frigate Constitution, Department of the United States Navy. (No other publication information)

U.S. Bureau of Naval Personnel. Commissaryman 3 & 2. U.S. Government Printing Office, Washington. 1948.

U.S. Department of Commerce. Armed Forces Recipe Service. U.S. Government Printing Office, Washington. 1992.

U.S. Navy Bureau of Supplies and Accounts. The Cook Book of the United States Navy. U. S. Government Printing Office, Washington. 1945.

U.S. Navy Department, Bureau of Navigation. Instructions for Use in Preparation for The Rating of Chief Commissary Steward. U.S. Government Printing Office, Washington. 1940.

Web Sites:

Civil War Interactive. "www.civilwarinteractive.com/"

Civil War Ironclads. "www.wideopenwest.com"

Civil War Navies Message Board. "http://history-sites.com/mb/cw/cwnavy"

Hyperwar: U.S. Navy in WWII. www.ibiblio.org/hyperwar/usn/

NavSource Online: Battleship Photo Archive. "www.navsource.org/archives"

Revolutionary War Message Board. "http://groups,yahoo.com/group.wwwrevwarcommessageboard/"

U.S. Naval Historic Center, Department of the Navy. "www.history.navy.mil/"